Thomas Merton attained fame for his writings on spirituality. To any who might wonder what he could contribute to the subject of liturgy, I can only recommend that they give this marvelous collection a chance. He has accomplished what we continue to struggle to do: reunite liturgy and spirituality, and make liturgy the fountain of life. He presents the best of the liturgical movement with a clarity and freshness that has lost none of its relevance since the time these articles were written. Each article stands fixed in the great tradition, while it simultaneously breathes the *aggiornamento* that the Second Vatican Council wished for the Church.

David Fagerberg
Associate Professor of Theology, Liturgical Studies
University of Notre Dame

Merton's writings are as important today as when they were originally published. Merton is concerned with showing how the liturgy breaks down dichotomies between temporal and spiritual worlds. In doing so, Merton makes clear that liturgical renewal is not something that can be imposed or legislated. Real liturgical renewal belongs to all members of the Church. It is the participation of every part of our lives in God's one cosmic liturgy. The more Merton's prose is formed by monastic life, the more it engages with the world beyond the monastery, combining the most realistic view of the world's ills with the greatest hope for redemption in the unfathomable depths of God's love.

William T. Cavanaugh
Professor of Theology
University of St. Thomas

A rich and remarkably relevant collection! Merton challenges Christians to be and become a community of worship, a community of pardon, a community called to ongoing reform and renewal in liturgy and life. For Merton, celebrating the seasons of the liturgical year is an invitation to enter ever more deeply into the mystery of life in Christ.

Christine M. Bochen
Editor of *Thomas Merton: Essential Writings*

Writing as a monk of a contemplative order and as a man fully alive to his times, [Merton] is able to combine, as in so much of his writing, the deep insight of a man of prayer with a keen and vigorous appreciation of liturgy as renewed today. In these essays he considers the major liturgical themes from Advent to Easter so that their eternal meaning and relevance is made clear. It is a book that belongs to the monastic life which experiences liturgy as the pivot of daily life wherein the community continually realizes the mysteries of the Kingdom as "God in Christ reconciling the world to Himself." It is the essential function of the monk to live the liturgy in this way; when a monk is also able to communicate this interior heart of the liturgy to his contemporaries, as Fr. Merton does here, he offers a way in which new and unfamiliar liturgical forms can become again "wells of living water, springing up into eternal life" (John 4:14).

Cardinal Basil Hume

The book is full of useful, helpful, valuable, penetrating comments.

Rev. Robert W. Hovda
The Critic

A quiet joy echoes from its pages, the alleluia of a man who has sensed the glory of the coming of the Lord.

The Catholic World

THOMAS MERTON

Seasons

— OF —

CELEBRATION

Meditations on the Cycle of Liturgical Feasts

ave maria press AMP notre dame, indiana

Acknowledgment is made to the editors of *Commonweal*, *The Critic*, and *Worship*, in whose pages some of these articles first appeared in somewhat different form.

Ex parte Ordinis
Nihil obstat
Fr. Charles English
Fr. Shane Regan

Imprimi potest
Fr. Ignace Gillet, Abbot General
Nihil obstat
Austin B. Vaughan, S.T.D.
Imprimatur
Terence J. Cooke, Vicar General, Archdiocese of New York

The nihil obstat and imprimatur are official declarations that a book or pamphlet is free of doctrinal or moral error. No implication is contained therein that those who have granted the nihil obstat and imprimatur agree with the contents, opinions or statements expressed.

Founded in 1865, Ave Maria Press is a ministry of the Indiana Province of Holy Cross.

www.avemariapress.com

ISBN-10 1-59471-170-4 ISBN-13 978-1-59471-170-1

Cover image © Corbis Images .

Cover and text design by Brian C. Conley.

Printed and bound in the United States of America.

CONTENTS

FOREWORD

Seasons of Celebration was published in 1965. The date is important, for 1965 marks the ending of the four-year Vatican II Council—arguably the most significant church council since the mid-first century "Council" of Jerusalem. For as that earlier council had done, Vatican II moved the Church in strikingly new directions. Like many of his co-religionists, Thomas Merton was swept up in the spirit of euphoria generated by the council.

The fifteen chapters that make up this book include addresses given at Gethsemani and articles published earlier in various journals: seven of the chapters date from the 1950s, eight from the 1960s (1950 being the earliest, 1964 the latest).

In *Seasons of Celebration*, Merton writes about the renewal and reform of the liturgy envisioned by Vatican II. In the first and last chapters of this book, he highlights specific insights from the council's *Constitution on the Sacred Liturgy*. This document was approved by the council fathers in 1963 and was, therefore, available for him to quote from before his manuscript went to publication. This he does in the first and last chapters. These two chapters may be thought of as two literary bookends dealing explicitly with the very nature and meaning of liturgy. They enclose thirteen additional chapters that in one way or another can be related to an understanding of liturgy, some more closely than others. (Chapter 3, "Time and the Liturgy," though written in 1955, is probably the closest to these two.) Of the thirteen other chapters, six have to do with the two great seasons (or cycles) of the liturgical calendar: three about the Advent-Christmas cycle; three others, the Lent-Easter cycle. The remaining chapters develop themes that can easily be linked with the spirit that should characterize liturgy.

This book is but one example of the amazing contemporaneity of Thomas Merton's writings. For what he wrote about liturgy continues to speak meaningfully to women and men today, more than forty years after the close of the Second Vatican Council. I guarantee that anyone reading this book today, whatever their knowledge of liturgy may have been before, will emerge from the reading with their grasp of liturgy and the cycles of the liturgical year expanded and deepened.

Liturgy, Merton emphasizes, is not a performance by "a group of specialists in the presence of passive spectators." We could put it this way: liturgy is not the priest's "thing" that the rest of us watch. It is rather the celebration of the whole Body of Christ, priest and people. It would be an overstatement to say that the Second Vatican Council took the Mass away from the priest and gave it back to the laity. It would be fair, however, to state that it did end what might be called the liturgical "monopoly" of the priest. In the liturgy we who are baptized into Christ—all of us—celebrate our participation in the mystery of Christ's redeeming presence. We celebrate not simply that we are *saved*, but the love that saves us. Liturgy is also the experience of *enlightenment* regarding the mystery of Christ and our oneness with him and in him with one another. At the same time liturgy helps in the process of our being *transformed* into the likeness of Christ.

The guarantee I offered earlier for this book I would apply in a special way to the chapters that deal with the two great liturgical cycles: Advent-Christmas and Lent-Easter.

They are the parts of this book that I find myself returning to with some regularity. Let me quote a few "gems" from these chapters. "The fact that the world is other than it might be does not alter the truth that Christ is present in it and that His plan has been neither frustrated nor changed: indeed, all will be done according to His will. Our Advent is the celebration of this hope." "Christ is born. . . . Today eternity enters into time and time, sanctified, is caught up into eternity. Today Christ, the eternal Word of the Father . . . enters into the world which He created in order to reclaim souls who had forgotten their identity." "Lent is not a season of punishment so much as one of healing." "Penance is conceived by the Church less as a burden than as a liberation." "The God of Ash Wednesday is like a calm sea of mercy. In Him there is no anger." "The power of Easter has burst upon us with the resurrection of Christ. Now we find in ourselves a strength which is not our own, and which is freely given to us whenever we need it, raising us above the Law, giving us a new law which is hidden in Christ: the law of His merciful love for us. Now we no longer strive to be good because we have to . . . but because our joy is to please Him who has given all His love to us. Now our life is full of meaning."

****

In 1967 Merton made a graph evaluating his books. *Seasons of Celebration* (with two other works) he classified as "Poor." It is difficult to understand his reasons for so low a classification for *Seasons*. Perhaps the reason may have been his expressed feeling that he had written too much. In a letter to James Baker, written in 1968, he said of his writings: "I must admit I really wish I had never written most of it." That same year he wrote to Sister Joan Marie: "Looking back on my work, I wish I had never bothered to write about one-third of it. . . . "

Certainly Merton had every right to classify his writings as he chose. But I strongly disagree with his classification of *Seasons of Celebration* as "Poor." Its value is such that it deserves a far better rating than he was willing to give it. I am confident, moreover, that others who read this book will agree with me.

Quite satisfied with my critique of Merton, I was somewhat taken aback when a colleague came up with another graph—also from 1967—that Merton had drawn up. In this graph two of the three books that had received a "Poor" evaluation remained in that category. The third one, however, *Seasons of Celebration,* was given a new designation. It was listed as "Good"!

William H. Shannon
Rochester, New York
January 2009

AUTHOR'S NOTE

These essays and addresses on the Liturgy were not merely composed in a monastic cell in order to be placed silently in the hands of a reader. Apart from two of the chapters that were written specifically at the request of magazines, everything in this book has been delivered to, and in some cases discussed with, a group or congregation.

The reader must obviously expect certain changes of tone and tempo, depending on when the matter was delivered, and to whom. The audience has varied from theological and philosophical students to Cistercian Novices and the Monastic Community of which the author is a member. A few chapters will bear the mark of identification imposed by the group to which they were given (for instance, *The Sacrament of Advent in St. Bernard*—to students of Patristic theology in 1952—and no effort was made to change the character of this theological conference). Most of them, however, are contemporary, universal and, one hopes, cogent.

The more recent articles are, obviously, the ones that come closer to saying what the author really wants to say. Three in particular represent most articulately his current concerns, *The Liturgy and Spiritual Personalism; Easter, The New Life;* and *The Good Samaritan.* These may prove to be controversial sections of a book that nowhere lays claim to a merely safe and conventional piety.

A final chapter takes stock of the current renewal in Liturgy and the conflicts it has aroused.

Abbey of Gethsemani, Kentucky
August 1965

LITURGY AND SPIRITUAL PERSONALISM

1. *The Personal Aspect of Liturgical Renewal*

The Second Vatican Council, while recalling that the liturgical worship of the Church "accomplishes the work of our Redemption," especially emphasizes the fact that the Liturgy is the chief means "whereby the faithful may express in their lives and manifest to others the mystery of Christ and the real nature of the true Church" (*Constitution on Liturgy,* Introduction, n. 2). For this reason the Council attaches very great importance to liturgical renewal, considering it to be essential to the frankly admitted aim of the Council: the reform of the entire Church by a renewal of Catholic life in all its depth and all its manifestations. This renewal is itself essential for another aim expressed by the Council "to promote union among all who believe in Christ; to strengthen whatever can help to call the whole of mankind into the household of the Church" (Ibid., n. 1).

The *Constitution on Liturgy* does not merely show the Church's approval of what has already been done by the Liturgical Movement. It is the beginning of a broad and general

Liturgical reform which, it is hoped, will accomplish the most striking and significant changes in every form of Catholic Worship. This is to be, and in fact already is, the greatest development in liturgy since the Patristic age and the most thorough reform in liturgy the Church has ever known.

This reform starts from a basic idea of the nature of Liturgy as public worship, as an activity of the Church carried out by Christ Himself in union with His Church. The very nature of this activity demands the "full, conscious and active participation of all the faithful." Not only that, but the task of bringing every Catholic to participate actively in Liturgical Worship is one that takes priority over everything else since a liturgical reform imposed by means of constraint from above would lack all genuine significance. Indeed no such authoritarian reform is envisaged by the Council. On the contrary, the *Constitution on Liturgy* foresees that the great liturgical renewal is to be carried out by the faithful themselves— Bishops, clergy and also laity. Therefore "in the restoration and promotion of the Sacred Liturgy this full and active participation by all the people is the aim to be considered before all else."

The present essay is concerned with the meaning of liturgical renewal not only as participation in new modes of worship, but as the creative joint effort of all Catholics to attain a new understanding of worship itself.

Liturgy is not just the fulfilment of a natural duty. It is the celebration of our unity in the Redemptive Love and Mystery of Christ. It is the expression of the self-awareness of a redeemed people. If the people themselves are not aware of their status and of their nobility as sons of God in Christ, how can they convincingly affirm and exercise their full spiritual rights as citizens in the Kingdom of God?

To understand this we have to go back to the classic Greek concept of Liturgy.

Liturgy is, in the original and classical sense of the word, a *political* activity. *Leitourgia* was a "public work," a contribution made by a free citizen of the *polis* to the celebration and manifestation of the visible life of the *polis*. As such it was distinct from the *economic* activity or the private and more material concern of making a living and managing the productive enterprises of the "household." Political life was the public and responsible domain of the free citizen—and was restricted to him alone.

Private life was properly the realm of those who were not considered to be fully "persons," like women, children and slaves, whose appearance in public was without significance because they had no ability to participate in the life of the city. As far as public life was concerned, they did not exist. In the days of the Athenian republic, public activity was at the same time political and religious, since the life of the city-state was basically religious.

The earliest notion of liturgy does not rest on a distinction between "sacred" and "secular." An example of "liturgy" in the Athenian democracy, would be the act of providing for the dithyrambic dance and procession, or the representation of the religious drama-cycle which developed out of the dithyramb. Note that here too, "art," "culture," and "religion" all coalesce in *Leitourgia*.

It is important, for our present purpose, to replace the term "liturgy" in its classical, hellenic context, where it is most clear and meaningful. Liturgical celebration in this ancient and original sense is a sacred and public action in which the community, at once religious and political, acknowledges its identity in worship.

This is essential for our theme, "Liturgy and spiritual personalism." Unless we begin by returning to the root meaning of liturgy, we will be led astray by the repercussions and confusions of modern controversy. Indeed, the superficial opposition so often created between liturgical prayer and "personal" prayer—an opposition which has no basis in reality—makes all genuine understanding of either liturgy or meditation practically impossible: as if liturgy were thinkable without some meditation, and as if meditation did not presuppose and complement the liturgical celebration of the mysteries of our redemption. Liturgical prayer is, or should be, eminently personal *because* it is public. To judge by polemical statements made on one side or the other one would almost imagine that there were thought to be two opposing ways of prayer and Christian fulfillment: the one exclusively public and corporate and the other exclusively private and individual. No wonder that the results are confusing! In the Christian city, *every* mature individual is a free citizen; no one is prevented by a servile condition from participating in the life on the *polis*, the Holy City, or better, the People of God. Each person, as a member of Christ, has a voice in the public worship of the Church, in that *"leitourgia"* which is the most exalted and most excellent of "public works" and which is at the same time the most perfect expression of the "economy" of that household which is the family not only of man but of the Heavenly Father. In this family none are slaves, all are "sons" and all have the privilege of free and spontaneous speech (*parrhesia*) in the Father's Presence, either alone or in the company of the other children and heirs of the Creator.

Therefore in this essay we are not trying to settle the largely misleading dispute about "public" and "private" prayer. We are not concerned with it at all. Rather, we are concerned with liturgical worship as the action of fully developed Christian persons, free citizens of the Christian *polis*, which is the City and house of God, the Church, the Mystical Body of Christ. Liturgy is an expression of their personality because in it they affirm their divine sonship and exercise their rights of citizenship in the heavenly Jerusalem; the eschatalogical and redeemed community of those who are one in Love, freed from the bonds of sin and death.

2. *Public Service*

It is our contention that unless the liturgy is the activity of free and mature persons, intelligently participating together in the corporate *cultus* which expresses and constitutes their visible spiritual society, it cannot have a real spiritual meaning. That is to say, of course, that from the moment corporate worship ceases to be genuinely *communal* and becomes, instead merely *collective*—as soon as it ceases to be the *collaboration of free persons*, each offering his own irreplaceable contribution, and becomes the mechanical functioning of anonymous units, whose identity and individual contribution are of no special worth—then it loses its right to be called liturgy of Christian worship. It is no longer the public witness of free and responsible personalities—it has become a demonstration by mass-men, or slaves.

It is true that the Lord in the Gospel speaks of His faithful as "sheep," but that does not entitle us to assume that the liturgy is merely the organized bleating of irrational animals herded together by constraint and trained by an ingenious discipline until they can carry out seemingly human actions which they are not capable of understanding.

On the other hand, liturgy in the full sense of the word cannot be merely the performance of a group of specialists in the presence of passive spectators. It is not merely theater. Liturgy demands the intelligent and active participation of all the mature members of the Assembly. The only spectators and "listeners" are the catechumens or public sinners who join in the liturgy of the word, the foremass, in which presumably all participate by listening and responding, each according to his ability. After this, the catechumens originally left the Assembly, though today they remain as "spectators." But this does not mean that the faithful are mere spectators like the catechumens. They have work to do. They are free citizens, and they have something very important to say in what is going on. They have responded to a divine summons. They are in a broad sense "celebrating," together with the officially deputed ministers, the mystery which expresses the unity and the solidarity of all the members of the One Christ. They participate in the eucharistic sacrifice by sacramental communion, and by all the rites and symbolic actions which manifest their grasp of the meaning of what they do, thus bearing witness to their faith and charity. They vocally express their presence and active consent by responses and chants. They bring their gifts to the altar. They join together in the sacred meal in which Christ gives them His Body and Blood to unite them in His love. This is their active share in the mystery.

From the very first moment in which a man becomes a Christian and begins to express himself as a vocal and active member of the Body of Christ, the liturgy reminds him of his personal and we might say "political" responsibility in the City of God. The Church is the Assembly of those who have been called together by God. As the catechumen approaches the font, the liturgy asks him his name, and demands that he declare freely and personally what he seeks from the Church. On the threshold of his new life, the catechumen declares that he, as an individual, has responded to the personal vocation, the call of Christ to enter into the Christian *polis* and to labor together with the other members of the Church to establish the reign of Christ's holiness, of the Holy Spirit, upon the earth, and to strive to bring all other men together with himself into eternal life.

Every liturgical act implies a renewed awakening of this basic Christian consciousness, and a fresh acceptance of this primal and personal responsibility. The Eucharist, the fulness of the Christian life and the center of Christian liturgy, is the great communal act by which the mystery of salvation is celebrated by the Church, and by her members, personally, together with her. It is the mystery in which Christ Himself, invisibly present in the midst of His faithful, spontaneously assisted by their free and sanctified love, and acclaimed by their unanimous consent, accomplishes His work of Redemption, announcing the full establishment of His Kingdom and sharing with all the fruits of salvation. The Second Vatican Council has stated this in the following terms:

> The Liturgy through which the work of our redemption is accomplished . . . is the outstanding means whereby the faithful may express in their lives and manifest to others the mystery of Christ and the true nature of the Church. (*Constitution on Liturgy*, Introduction, n. 2)

The Council especially emphasizes the presence of Christ in the assembly of the faithful called together by Him to celebrate with Him the liturgical mysteries:

> Christ is always present in His Church, especially in her liturgical celebrations;
> Christ always associates the Church with Himself in this great work wherein God is perfectly glorified and men are sanctified;
> In the Liturgy the whole public worship is performed by the Mystical Body of Jesus Christ, that is, by the Head and His members. (*Idem.*, Chapter I, n. 7)

Hence it is altogether insufficient to treat the liturgy merely as the corporate expression of "subjection" which man as a social being owes to God as his Creator. Although correct, this is far too abstract an expression of the liturgical mystery. It is incomplete first of all in reducing liturgical worship to an ethical concept. It also leads to the misconception that liturgy is worship carried out by "society," by "the group" *as opposed to* the individuals who compose the group. Hence the confusing deduction that the individual's chief function is to lose himself, to submerge himself, to divest himself of every trace of individuality and personality in order to vanish into the group, so that in this way the collectivity may more perfectly express its subjection to God. The individual subjects himself to the group by prostrating himself and vanishing from sight, and the group prostrates itself before God. In this way society as such, in the abstract, pays a debt due in justice to God.

According to this conception, the Christian life is primarily one of *servitude*. But we must remember that according to our classical analogy of *leitourgia*, liturgy and servitude are mutually exclusive. A slave cannot offer public service because he is not free or responsible and has no way of making his entry into the public realm. He is a non-person. And liturgy is by no means a parade or demonstration of non-persons! To say that liturgy gives glory to God by the abject submission of slaves is, as a matter of fact, to misunderstand the real Biblical notion of the glory of God.

The glory of God is the effulgence of His own presence manifested in mystery, and men "give Him glory" by the sacred awe and the spontaneous exultation, with which they recognize and acclaim His presence in fear, trembling and holy joy. It is the freedom of man and his free submission to God in love that "give glory to God." What glorifies God, in man's submission to God, is not the fact of submission alone, but the far deeper truth that by submitting to God man gains his freedom. By "renouncing" his private and "economic" self for love of God man finds his true self. This is one of the characteristic experiences of Liturgical worship which purifies and ennobles those who participate in the objectivity and sacredness of the common celebration, even where this may mean a certain sacrifice of intimacy and subjective warmth. Actually, the loss is only apparent. The growth of freedom in divine service brings with it a more mature fervor and deeper capacity for the inner awareness of God's love, manifested to the worshipping community in the sacred mysteries.

In the sacred liturgy, therefore, the faithful act not as mere spectators, as inert and passive figures, or as servants and slaves. The liturgy everywhere implies awareness that we are the friends and collaborators with Christ in His great work of Redeeming and sanctifying the entire cosmos. The Lord

Himself sets great store by this awareness and He has explicitly affirmed His desire for it. "I do not speak of you any more as my servants; a servant is one who does not understand what his master is about, whereas I have made known to you all that my Father has told me; and so I have called you my friends. It was not you that chose me, it was I that chose you. The task I have appointed you is to go out and bear fruit, fruit which will endure; so that every request you make of the Father in my name may be granted you. These are the directions I give you, that you should love one another" (John 15:15–17, Knox Version).

3. *A Royal Priesthood*

Hence we can easily understand the words of St. Peter to the laity, the *laos*, the people of God, the citizens of the Holy City: "You are a chosen race, a royal priesthood, a consecrated nation, a people God means to have for Himself; it is yours to proclaim the exploits of the God who has called you out of darkness into His marvelous light. Time was when you were not a people at all, now you are God's people; once you were unpitied, now pity is yours" (I Peter 2:9–10).

Here we have one of the innumerable texts of the New Testament which gives us in a few words the whole *politeia* of the Christian person in the City of God. His personal dignity, his freedom, his citizenship in the holy people, are the gift of God. His citizenship has been received by a personal response to a personal calling. The "political activity" of the holy People, which is centered mainly in the liturgy, consists in "proclaiming the exploits" of the God of mercy, the Redeemer and sanctifier of man and in sharing, by love and sacrifice, in His work of Redemption. The highest personal and spiritual dignity of the Christian is his participation by baptism in the priesthood and sonship of Christ: this of course surpassed by the even greater dignity of sacramental ordination in which certain Christians are anointed and signed with the priestly character to consecrate the sacrificial offering in the name and Person of Christ. But this does not mean that they are to carry out the liturgy alone and unaided, with the people present only as mute and passive spectators. On the contrary, it is upon *all* that the obligation falls to proclaim the great works of God, the *magnalia Dei,* since all alike, without distinction, have been called out of darkness into His admirable light.

The distinction between priest and people which is so evident in the sacramental liturgy is less emphatic in the liturgy of the Word, and for that reason it is very much to be desired that all the faithful once again fulfill active roles which have for centuries been restricted in various ways. All can participate in singing and some may read the sacred texts to the others. The Council states that the layman should have an "office to perform" in the liturgical celebration (Chapter I, nn. 28, 29, 30). In fact the Council encourages Bible services to be conducted by deacons or by lay-people approved by the Bishop, not only on vigils or on weekdays in Advent and Lent, but also on Sundays, especially where no priest is available for Mass. These Bible services are liturgical celebrations, not mere para-liturgical devotions (see Chapter I, n. 35). Note that laymen will play an active part in the Institutes of Pastoral Liturgy which the Council foresees as an important element in the work of liturgical reform (Chapter I, n. 44).

Both the Old and New Testaments repeatedly affirm that freedom is the characteristic of the member of the People of God. As a matter of fact, this People first came into existence when the children of Israel were delivered from slavery in Egypt and called out into the desert to be educated in freedom, to learn how to live with no other Master but God Himself. The crossing of the Red Sea was, however, only a prophetic type of the final freedom that was to be conferred upon those who shared in the *pascha Christi,* the "passover" in which Christ "crossed over" from death to life and from this world to the Father.

Just as in a civic holiday a political community renews its awareness of its own identity, affirming its character by recalling and celebrating its origin and its special achievements, so in Liturgy the members of the supernatural *politeia*, the citizens of the City of God and members of the Body of Christ, affirm their character by proclaiming their faith in the acts by which God, entering into history created for Himself a holy people.

The difference between a civic and liturgical celebration is that the latter is concerned with a radically different aspect of history—a totally different kind of event. Liturgy is centered on a divine event in human history, the entrance of a saving and transforming power into the life and the affairs of men. As St. Gregory Nazianzen says: "We celebrate not our sickness but our cure" (*Oratio* 38).

The liturgy is precisely the public act by which the whole Church reenacts the Christian pasch, the passage from death to life in the mystery of the death and resurrection of Christ. In so doing, the faithful Assembly, and each individual member of the Assembly, recognizes the permanent, undying efficacy of the great salvific act of the Redeemer, which is the guarantee of each Christian's individual spiritual freedom, and at the same time constitutes the People of God. We must remember that the liturgy does much more than merely *commemorate* the sacred redemptive mystery. On the contrary, it is the privilege of each member of the sacred Assembly to *co-operate* with the Church and with God Himself, in some manner, in the celebration of the sacred mystery. Hence active participation in the liturgy means not only an intelligent following of what is done by the sacred ministers, but far more than that—a spiritual co-operation in the very work of God Himself as the Head and Ruler of the Holy City. In the words of Pope Pius XII:

> Marvelous though it appear, Christ requires
> His members. . . . In carrying out the work of
> Redemption, Christ wishes to be helped by the

members of His Body. This is not because He
is indigent and weak but rather because He so
willed it for the greater glory of His unspotted
Spouse. Dying on the Cross He left to His Church
the immense treasury of the Redemption; toward
this she contributed nothing. But when those
graces come to be distributed, not only does He
share this task of sanctification with His Church
but He wants it in a way to be due to her action.
(*Mystici Corporis*)

It is of course to be clearly understood that man's co-
operation with God in the divine mysteries takes place on
very different levels. We all "work with" God as members of
Christ, but there are different degrees in which we share in
the priesthood of Christ. The baptized faithful offer the holy
sacrifice in union with the ordained priest, but in a different
sense. He offers it by virtue of his priestly power, as a mediator and representative of Christ. They offer it by uniting their
prayers and desires with His. In the words of Innocent III,
quoted by Pius XII in *Mediator Dei*, "What the priest does personally by virtue of his ministry, the faithful do collectively by
virtue of their intention." Hence the laity are not priests in the
strict sense of the word. But it is clear from the Vatican Council and the great modern encyclicals that liturgical activity of
the faithful, their participation in the sacred mysteries, is by
no means supposed to be passive, inarticulate, a mere matter of "receiving" grace. On the contrary, they offer sacrifice,
and in this offering the Covenant between God and His people is renewed. This is the highest expression of the Church's
communal life as well as of the Christian's personal dedication. Indeed the Catholic believes this to be the most significant and indeed the most sublime act possible to man, for it is
the expression of that love in which God draws man to Himself in order to share with him a life and light that infinitely
transcend man's nature. But the renewal of the covenant in

the Eucharistic sacrifice demands the free and intelligent co-operation of all the people of God.

The Second Vatican Council has emphatically rejected the mentality that has been characterized half-humorously by the word "validism." This is a view of liturgy which concentrates on the exact fulfillment of rubrical prescriptions by the priest, in order that certain guaranteed effects may be produced in the faithful *ex opere operato*. This requires nothing more than minimal dispositions in the faithful, amounting to their physical presence and the essentials of good will. The Council says:

> Pastors of souls must therefore realize that when the liturgy is celebrated, something more is required than the mere observation of the laws governing valid and licit celebration; it is their duty also to ensure that the faithful take part fully aware of what they are doing, *actively engaged in the rite and enriched by its effects.* (Chapter I, n. 11)

Hence, as the Council makes clear (Chapter I, n. 14.), the very nature of the Liturgy demands "the full, conscious and active participations of all the faithful." This teaching had already been brought out sixteen years before by Pope Pius XII in *Mediator Dei:*

> It is desirable that all the faithful should be aware that to participate in the Eucharistic sacrifice is their chief duty and supreme dignity, and that not in an inert and negligent fashion, giving way to distractions and day dreaming but with such earnestness and concentration that they may be united as closely as possible with the High Priest according to the Apostle: "Let this mind be in you which was also in Christ Jesus." *And together with Him and through Him let them make their oblation, and in union with Him let them offer up themselves.* (*Mediator Dei*)

For all the members of the sacred Assembly, mature participation in the liturgical worship of the Church implies a high level of spiritual freedom, responsibility, understanding and even wisdom. This is true of *all the faithful.* It may be an ideal that sometimes falls far short of realization. But certainly in the priest himself, trained and consecrated for the sacred ministry, we must expect to find that depth of understanding, that fully developed spiritual personality, that maturity in the liturgical life which implies a deep and humble awareness of his mission and of the fact that he is not only a "person" in his own right but "another Christ," appointed to represent the Risen Savior and to "act in the person of Christ." Surely the priesthood demands a high degree of Christian personalism. Such personalism is more than professional poise, or official competence. It implies holiness of life, profound humility, and a selflessness which leaves the priest capable of faithful and enlightened obedience to the Holy Spirit.

If the priest is, in this highest and most perfect sense, a Christian "person," then there is more chance that the liturgy over which he presides and in which he officiates will be carried out in a similar spirit of personal and enlightened participation by the faithful. This is not merely a matter of liturgical "zeal" or of enthusiastic promotion of ceremonies. We must be on our guard against a kind of blind and immature zeal— the zeal of the enthusiast or of the zealot—which represents precisely a frantic compensation for the deeply personal qualities which are lacking to us. The zealot is a man who "loses himself" in his cause in such a way that he can no longer "find himself" at all. Yet paradoxically this "loss" of himself is not the salutary self-forgetfulness commanded by Christ. It is rather an immersion in his own wilfulness conceived as the will of an abstract, non-personal force: the force of a project or a program. He is, in other words, alienated by the violence of his own enthusiasm: and by that very violence he tends to produce the same kind of alienation in others. This type of zeal does great harm to the liturgy. It tends to offend the good sense and taste of those who seek in liturgical worship much more than a "cause" or a "program." They seek their full dignity as free participants in a sacred, public act directed to God alone—seeking His glory and not the glory and satisfaction of men.

Certainly the strong emphasis of the Vatican Council on liturgical reform will lend a new perspective to this zeal for new directions in worship. It is no longer a question of a "liturgical movement" in the sense of a "cause" espoused by an enlightened minority, and in which general interest remains optional. The Council has declared that liturgical reform is essential to the reform of the Church itself, and that the active participation of all the faithful in the Liturgy is essential to liturgical reform.

This brings out what we have said about the "political" character of liturgical participation, with the word "political" being used in a special sense—the activity of concerned citizens of the city (or *polis*) of the Church.

The faithful Christian who participates actively in liturgical reform is in fact playing a very important and active part in the public or "political" life of the Church. He is offering his personal contribution to the great work of Christian renewal undertaken by the Council.

In one word, to participate intelligently in liturgical worship is now to participate actively in the reform of the whole Church.

4. True and False Personalism

If individualism and subjectivism are so widely suspect among us, there is perhaps a very good reason for it. We live in a climate of individualism. But our individualism is in decay. Our tradition of freedom which, as a matter of fact, is rooted in a deeply Christian soil, and which in itself is worthy of the highest respect and loyalty, has begun to lose its genuine vitality. It is becoming more and more a verbal convention rather than a spiritual conviction. The tendency to substitute words about freedom for the reality of freedom itself has brought us to a state of ambivalent spiritual servitude. The noise with which we protest our love of freedom tends to be proportionate to our actual fear of genuine freedom, and our guilt at our unconscious refusal to pay the price of freedom. The agitated and querulous license with which we abandon ourselves to our own fantasies is a purely subjective and fallacious excuse for freedom.

The illusory character of the freedom which we have tried to find in moral and psychological irresponsibility, has become inescapable. Our abdication of responsibility is at the same time an abdication of liberty. The resolution to let "someone else," the anonymous forces of society, assume responsibility for everything means that we abdicate from public responsibility, from mature concern, and even from spiritual life. We retire from the public realm of freedom into the private world of necessity, imagining that the escape from responsibility is an escape into freedom. On the contrary, it is, in Erich Fromm's words, an "escape *from* freedom." But when we turn over the running of our lives to anonymous forces, to "them" (whoever "they" may be, and nobody quite knows), what actually happens is that we fall under the tyranny of collective fantasies and delusions. There is no more tyrannical dictator than convention, fashion, and prejudice.

We are beginning to understand that we live in a climate of all-embracing conformities. We have become mass-produced automatons. Our lives, our homes, our cities, our thoughts, or perhaps our lack of thoughts, have all taken on an impersonal mask of resigned and monotonous sameness. We who once made such a cult of originality, experiment, personal commitment and individual creativity, now find ourselves among the least individual, the least original and the least personal of all the people on the face of the earth—not excluding the Russians. In this desperate situation, the ideal of individuality has not been laid aside. Rather it has taken on the features of an obsessive cult. People "express themselves" in ways that grow more and more frantic in proportion as they realize that the individuality and the distinctive difference they are attempting to express no longer exist. To adapt the old French proverb, the more we try to express our difference by "originality," the more we show that we are the same: *plus ça change, plus c'est la même chose.* There is nothing so monotonously unoriginal as the capricious eccentricities of atoms in a mass-society.

What is the real root of personality in a man? It is obviously that which is *irreplaceable,* genuinely unique, on the deepest spiritual level. *Personalism* is the discovery, the *respect,* but not the *cult,* for this deep reality. Secular personalism is a kind of craze for individuality, a rage for self-manifestation in which the highest value is sought in the *recognition* by others of one's own uniqueness.

But the great paradox of Christian personalism is this: it consists in something more than bringing to light the unique and irreplaceable element in the individual Christian.

On the contrary, Christian personalism does not require that the inmost secret of our being become manifest or public to all. We do not even have to see it clearly ourselves. We are more truly "Christian persons" when our inmost secret remains a mystery shared by ourselves and God, and communicated to others in a way that is at the same time secret and public.

In other words, Christian personalism does not root out the inner secret of the individual in order to put it on display in a spiritual beauty-contest. On the contrary, our growing awareness of our own personality enables us at the same time to divine and to respect the inner secret of our neighbor, our brother in Christ.

Christian personalism is, then, the sacramental sharing of the inner secret of personality in the mystery of love. This sharing demands full respect for the mystery of the person, whether it be our own person, or the person of our neighbor, or the infinite secret of God. In fact, Christian personalism is the discovery of one's own inmost self, and of the inmost self of one's neighbor, in the mystery of Christ: a discovery that respects the hiddenness and incommunicability of each one's personal secret, while paying tribute to his presence in the common celebration.

Now it is precisely in the liturgy, the *public* prayer of the Christian Assembly, that the Christian best discovers the secret of his own inviolable solitude, and learns to respect the solitude of his brother while at the same time sharing it. This is not possible without the *public* celebration of the mysteries: public of course to the faithful assembly, though not necessarily to the uninitiated.

The Christian person finds himself and his brother in the *communal celebration of the mystery of Christ*. But what is manifested, proclaimed, celebrated and consummated in the liturgy is not *my* personality or *your* personality: it is the personality of Christ the Lord who, when two or three of us are gathered together in His Name, *is present in the midst of us*. This presence of Christ in the liturgical celebration leads to our discovery and declaration of our own secret and spiritual self.

But let us above all remember and admire the discretion, the sobriety and the modesty with which the liturgy protects this personal witness of the individual Christian. In the celebration of the liturgy, each one of us should give his personal and unique response to the call of God, the word addressed to him by the Lord in and through the Church. Yet this witness of our own inmost self, given publicly with complete honesty and sincerity, nevertheless remains "secret." Our spiritual modesty is protected by the reserve, the universality and in some sense the objective "impersonality" of the liturgical action.

Far from displaying a "characteristic difference," far from "standing out" as "unusual" by reason of our gifts, our style, and our "personality" in the popular sense of the word, we approach the sacraments with disciplined reserve. We sing alike, we pray alike, we adopt the same attitudes. Yet oddly enough this "sameness" does not wound our individuality; certainly it does nothing to diminish our fervor. On the contrary, it is the providential guarantee of a chaste, spiritual enthusiasm which is all the more pure because it does not have to display itself, or even be aware of itself at all!

The liturgy, then, is public: but not in the sense that a market place is public. Our singing, our attitudes, our personal testimony, are not put on display as it were for sale, for their market value. We are not trading our inmost secret for anything: for approval, for consolation, for ambition's sake, for self-gratification.

"What shall a man give in exchange for his soul?" That sentence is the very heart of Christian personalism. Our soul is irreplaceable, it can be exchanged for *nothing* in heaven or on earth, but until we have heard Christ speak, until we have received His call from the midst of the Christian Assembly (every vocation to the faith comes at least implicitly through the Church) and until we have given to Him that secret and unique answer which no one can pronounce in our place, until we have thus found ourselves in Him, we cannot fully realize what it means to be a "person" in the deepest sense of the word.

Until we have found Christ and entered into the true spirit of the liturgy there will always be the temptation to "sell our soul." There will always be a depraved urge, excited by the contagiousness of secular mendacity, to pry into our inmost secret, to put our superficial self on display, inviting others to manifest what is unique in us by offering to "buy" it.

Secular personalism is therefore at the same time degrading and frustrating. It cheapens and betrays our soul by putting it on sale. It does so by its impertinent confusion of the public and private realms. It mistakes the "private" for the "irreplaceable" and invades the region in which we are weakest and most trivial in order to put our nonentity on display, to make it "public." At the same time it supposes that anyone who is tough enough to stand up under this violation is a genuine "person." This is our modern form of idolatry—a religion not fit for free men, because it enslaves.

In conclusion, it is precisely because it is public in the classical or "political" sense of the word, that the liturgy enables us to discover and to express the deepest meaning of Christian personalism. We must first emerge from the private realm, the "household" which is the realm of necessity and the proper domain of children and slaves who have not yet a mind of their own and who are therefore completely absorbed in their own bodily and emotional needs. We must be able to put aside the "economic" concern with our superficial selves, and emerge into the open light of the Christian *polis* where each one lives not for himself but for others, taking upon himself the responsibility for the whole. Of course no one assumes this responsibility merely in obedience to arbitrary whim or to the delusion that he is of himself capable of taking the troubles of the whole Assembly on his own shoulders. But he emerges "in Christ," to share the labor and worship of the whole Christ, and in order to do this he must *sacrifice* his own superficial and private self. The paradoxical fruit of this sacrifice of his trivial and "selfish" (or simply immature) self is that he is then enabled to discover his deep self, in Christ.

This discovery suggests a further step, which goes beyond the limits of liturgy in the strict sense of the word. The public life and worship of the Church are not yet all. There is contemplation, which is neither liturgy nor privacy, because it transcends them both.

The liturgy, as such, may lead to contemplation; but it is not yet contemplation, and those who proclaim that "the liturgy is the highest form of Christian contemplation" are in error. Or at least they should take the trouble to make a few distinctions that will clarify their meaning.

The liturgy is, as the Fathers taught, a work of the *active* life. It prepares us for contemplation, which is the final

perfection of Christian personalism since it is the intimate realization of one's perfect union with Christ "in one Spirit."
The highest paradox of Christian personalism is for an individual to be "found in Christ Jesus" and thus "lost" to all that
can be regarded, in a mundane way, as his "self." This means
to be at the same time one's self and Christ. But this is not to
be ascribed solely to personal initiative, "private prayer" or
individual effort. Contemplation is a gift of God, given in and
through His Church, and through the prayer of the Church.
St. Anthony was led into the desert not by a private voice but
by the word of God, proclaimed in the Church of his Egyp-
tian village in the chanting of the Gospel in Coptic—a classic
example of liturgy opening the way to a life of contemplation! But the liturgy cannot fulfill this function if we misunderstand or underestimate the essentially spiritual value of
Christian public prayer. If we cling to immature and limited
notions of "privacy" we will never be able to free ourselves
from the bonds of individualism. We will never realize how
the Church delivers us from ourselves by public worship, the
very public character of which tends to hide us "in the secret
of God's Face."

[1963]

Church and Bishop in
St. Ignatius of Antioch

"I am privileged to bear a name radiant with divine
*   splendor,*
*   and so in the chains which I carry about on me I sing*
*   the praises*
*   of the Churches,*
*   and pray for union in their midst,*
*   a union based on the flesh and spirit of Jesus Christ,*
*   our enduring life;*
*   a union based on faith and love, the greatest blessing;*
*   and most especially a union with Jesus and the*
*   Father.*
If in this union we patiently endure all the abuse of the
*   Prince of this world and escape unscathed,*
*   we shall happily make our way to God."*

These words were written in the year 107 AD by the bishop of Antioch, to the Church of the Magnesians. When he
wrote them on his way to martyrdom in Rome, he wrote in

the full consciousness of the splendor of the Christian and Episcopal vocation, the splendor of the Church of Christ. His was a profound experience of the mystery of Christ, an experience of a bishop and a martyr, almost a contemporary of the apostles, one who had perhaps personally known St. Peter, St. Paul and St. John.

It is from this full experience that the ecclesiology of St. Ignatius is born. Not a theory, not a doctrine only: this is the holy, solemn and hieratic proclamation of the greatest of all realities: the mystery of Christ in His Church. The one who proclaims it is a Bishop—a direct successor of the Apostles.

It is characteristic of some of the greatest writers, as it is of those who have entered most deeply into the mystery of Christ, that one finds on almost every page of their work paragraphs which contain, in clear summary, the whole heart of their message. It is so with Ignatius of Antioch. His whole ecclesiology, in fact his whole theology is contained in brief in this passage to the Magnesians.

His theology of the Church is a theology of *kerygma* and acclamation. It is not a collection of dogmatic theses but a liturgy, a hymn of praise, surrounding an act of sacrifice. He sings the praises of the Church, the Body of Christ, born from His true Body in His true Passion. For Ignatius emphasizes repeatedly the reality of Christ, flesh and spirit, in His historical presence, in His eucharistic presence, and His real presence in His Body the Church.

His theology is at the same time a hymn in honor of unity and a prayer for the confirmation of unity. By unity and solidarity in faith and love, the Church sustains all the attacks of the enemy, and so all the faithful members of Christ make their way securely out of this world to the Father.

Ignatius glories first of all in the privilege that is given to him, the place assigned to him in the Church and designated by a glorious name. Ignatius then was acutely conscious of the profound importance of his episcopal task. The unity of all races in Christ must manifest God to the world. The walls separating men on the basis of racial, national and social distinctions must be torn down. Jew and Gentile must be one in Christ. His function as bishop is then twofold: to break down the walls of division and to maintain unity in truth and charity. It is above all in the liturgical mystery that Christ is present and acts upon the faithful gathered in the liturgical assembly. It is there that He sanctifies and unites them, drawing them closer in the bonds of Christian *agape*, and thereby strengthening them with supernatural energy to resist the attacks of the enemies of unity.

What is this name "radiant with divine splendor"? Perhaps the name of bishop, for St. Ignatius was more deeply conscious than perhaps any other sainted bishop, of the true meaning of the episcopate. Perhaps the name of martyr, though he was not yet sure that this name would be his, and he prayed earnestly that it might be granted to him. Perhaps his own name of "Ignatius" the "man of fire." Most probably his cognomen of *Theophorus,* the "man who bears in himself God."

Ignatius was fully aware that as a Christian, as a priest, and above all as a bishop, he was filled with the glory of the Risen Christ. His vocation to martyrdom was the pledge of the imminent revelation of that glory in him, consummated in perfect and even visible union. For Ignatius and his contemporaries were convinced that the moment of martyrdom was the climax of the Christian life, and at that moment the sacred passion and resurrection of the Lord was made visible and manifest in His martyr, His witness, who entered, through the *Pascha Christi,* into perfect and undying union with the Risen Lord.

1. *The Church of Antioch*

Antioch was then the fourth city of the Empire, after Rome, Alexandria and Ctesiphon. It was a new metropolis, almost like a modern American city, laid out in rectangular squares. Rich, cosmopolitan, a city of commerce, of pleasure, a great military base: Chrysostom called Antioch a "whole world in itself." It needed an Apostle to be its bishop! Among the Jews segregated in the ghetto, the Church of Antioch had been founded by Christians who fled Jerusalem after the martyrdom of St. Stephen. Consolidated by Paul and Barnabas, Antioch became the first see of Peter, and thus acquired a very special dignity and importance, which it has never lost. Ignatius may even have been the first bishop after Peter. St. Chrysostom, himself bishop of Antioch, claims that Ignatius was ordained by Peter.

As bishop of Antioch, Ignatius faced very special problems: three grave sources of danger to the unity and holiness of his nascent Church,

1—The Judaizing Christians (conservatives) resented the admission of gentiles, and fought for the preservation of familiar Jewish rites. They threatened the living unity of the Church by their exclusiveness, rigidity and attachment to the past;

2—Pagans, with their loose morality, their cynicism, religious indifference, their contempt of Christians, threatened the Church with violent persecution and hatred;

3—Gnostics, docetists and other heretical sects threatened the unity of faith with false mysticism, and the unity of charity with wrangling and schism.

In 107 Ignatius crowned his episcopacy with sacrifice. He was condemned to death under Trajan. He was sent to Rome overland, visited Churches as he went, conferred with bishops, exhorted the faithful, wrote his epistles as processional hymns in preparation for sacrifice. He reached Rome in time for the end of a 23-day celebration of the conquest of Dacia. In this celebration some ten-thousand gladiators perished, eleven-thousand wild beasts were killed in the arena.

One of the Christians who died was Ignatius. We know his famous prayers in the Epistle to the Romans, and in the liturgy of his feast: "*sitos Christou eimi. . . .* I am the wheat of Christ: may I be ground by the teeth of the wild beasts so that

I may become pure bread." This is not only the voice of the martyr and witness to the Risen Christ, but also the voice of the bishop and witness to Christ living in the Mystery of His Church. It is the voice of a high priest, a man of the Church, a man of sacrifice, who clearly realizes that the Eucharist is the living and radiant center of the Mystery of the Church, for there Christ gathers all clergy and all the faithful about the bishop to unite them with His sacrifice, and share with them the fruit of His glorious victory.

2. *The Mystery of the Church*

The short epistles of St. Ignatius all share a common structure. They were written to be read in the liturgical assembly, and each one begins with a salutation of the Church to which it is addressed. These salutations are anything but the pompous and formal salutations of official Roman letters: they are lyrical improvisations, prophetic hymns in honor of the mystery of Christ in the Church—not just Christ in the Church as a whole, but also of Christ in each local Church, gathered around its bishop, as a witness to God's merciful and salvific love for men.

Each salutation shows clearly that for Ignatius each Church is a living being, or rather a part of the great living organism which is the Body of Christ. It is not just a social organization, it is a mystical person, alive with the presence of Christ. The Church is the manifestation of Christ Who, in turn, is the revelation of the Father. By the mystery of the Church the invisible God makes Himself known to the world.

After the salutation Ignatius usually goes on to exhort the faithful to reverence and obedience to their bishop, the visible representative of the invisible Christ present in their midst. He then outlines his teaching on the unity of the Church in Christ, the Church as the Body of Christ, united in one faith, one hope, one charity gathered about the bishops, presbyters and deacons.

Ignatius frequently refers to his own martyrdom, especially as a witness to the reality of Christ, the reality of the flesh and sufferings of Christ, the reality of the Eucharist. It is in martyrdom that Ignatius hopes to become a Christian in the full sense of one who has "found Christ" and become perfectly "united to Christ and to the Father."

He adds other exhortations, usually concerned with unity in obedience and love, meekness, and the avoidance of disputes. Above all he cautions the Christians against heresy. Humble and faithful union with their bishop and presbyters will be their guarantee against error and dissension. Let us now return to the salutations with which the epistles open. They are always the most lyrical and often the richest part of the letter. From these salutations alone we can draw an inexhaustible amount of material to reconstruct the ecclesiology of St. Ignatius.

Each Church is worthy of all praise, each is blessed, splendid, glorious, the "pleroma" of the divine love, predestined from all eternity, the object of an admirable choice made in Christ, by the Father. More particularly each Church is "chosen in the Passion." Each Church was the object of Christ's love of predilection as He died on the Cross, and hence is called to an ineffable dignity. Each must concentrate entirely on a worthy response of love, a deep realization of the loftiness of this calling, in the mystery of the Passion and of the Resurrection. Because each Church is so chosen, it is also illuminated, filled with a special light, the light of its vocation. It must be purified by that same light. It must cooperate in its own purification by the light. Cooperation consists in eliminating everything that brings about disunity in thought, in worship, and in love.

In proportion as each Church responds to this call, advances towards the light, dwells in unity in the grace of God, through Jesus Christ, it becomes a hymn of joy and praise, glorifying the Father by union with Him in Christ.

Thus, for instance, he salutes the Church of Philadelphia:

> *"A Church which has found mercy and is irrevocably of
> one mind with God;
> which unwaveringly exults in the Passion of Our Lord
> and firmly believes in His resurrection through sheer
> mercy.
> This Church I salute in the Blood of Jesus Christ.
> She is a source of everlasting joy, especially when her
> members are
> one with their Bishop."* (*Ad Phil.*, Prol.)

If anyone seeks Christ, if anyone seeks holiness, the way is clear. He must make his way to the community of the faithful. He must enter into the *agape,* the community of love, which is his local Church. He will find the Church, like that of Smyrna,

> *"Overflowing with faith and love
> lacking in no gift,
> Radiant with God's splendor and fruitful mother of
> saints."* (Smyr. Prol.)

Or read for example the wonderful salutation to the Church of Rome, "presiding in love":

> *"Ignatius, also called Theophorus,
> to the Church that has found mercy in the transcendent
> Majesty of the Most High Father
> and of Jesus Christ, His only Son;
> the Church by the will of Him who willed all things
> that exist,
> beloved and illuminated through the faith and love of
> Jesus Christ our God;
> which also presides in the chief place of the Roman
> territory;
> a Church worthy of God, worthy of honor, worthy of
> felicitation,*

worthy of praise, worthy of success
worthy of sanctification, and presiding in love,
maintaining the law of Christ, and bearer of the
*   Father's name:*
her do I therefore salute in the name of Jesus Christ, the
*   Son of the Father.*
Heartiest good wishes for unimpaired joy in Jesus
*   Christ our God,*
*   to those who are united in flesh and spirit by every*
*   commandment of His;*
who imperturbably enjoy the full measure of God's
*   grace*
and have every foreign stain filtered out of them." (*Ad*
*   Rom.,* Prol.)

3. *Una Sancta*

Of the four notes of the Church given in the Nicene creed, "one, holy, Catholic and apostolic," three are clearly developed by St. Ignatius. As for the fourth, apostolicity, it is to be sought in him implicitly rather than explicitly. He was too close to the Apostles to develop this note in detail and in perspective. But at the same time we must remember he was the greatest and most articulate of the Apostolic Fathers. His letters are full to overflowing with the doctrine taught by St. John and St. Paul. His life itself, all his words, his actions and his death are a living witness to the Apostolicity of the Church.

St. Ignatius is the very first to make use of the word "Catholic" in reference to the Church. The universal Church, which is the unity of all the Churches, is the *katholike*. It unites in itself all races and all peoples, for all are called to unity and peace in Christ. To exclude anyone because of race or social background is to strike at the living unity of the Body of Christ.

The Church is presided over by Christ Himself, Who also presides over each local Church. Christ is the Bishop of the whole Church, and the bishop of each local Church. But each Church also has its "visible bishop" who is simply the representative of Christ, invisibly present wherever the bishop himself is.

The Unity and Holiness of the Church shine forth on every page of the letters of Ignatius. They are the heart of his whole teaching. He calls himself "a man made for unity." He is the hymnodist of unity.

In particular he makes quite clear that unity and holiness go together. They are in direct proportion to one another. The more a Church is one with the Father and Jesus Christ, the more it shares their holiness, by participating in the source of all holiness which is the Passion of Christ.

However the invisible and spiritual unity of the faithful in Christ is inseparable from their union in the visible order established by Him. There is for Ignatius no contradiction between the "spiritual" and the "institutional" aspects of the Church. The reality of unity in Christ must be proved and verified by unity with the bishop and presbyters in belief, in worship, in love, for where the bishop is, there is Christ. Ignatius strongly affirms the hierarchical structure of the visible Church, and this is essential to his teaching on unity. The assembly of the faithful, united around the bishop in the liturgical sacrifice, is one with the crucified and Risen Christ and with Him offers itself in joy and glory to the Father.

Every influence, on the other hand, which leads to disunity leads also to corruption and to spiritual death. Not only that, but it obscures and effaces the life-giving presence of Christ! The Church is a body, a living body. It must be kept organically whole by the constant presence of Christ Himself, and where there is division, where love cools, then life fails, disintegration sets in. A Church torn by divisions would be a dying body. A Church completely divided, completely cut off from unity with the Head and source of life, would be a dead body, and it would smell of corruption. Instead of manifesting Christ to the world, it would manifest only falsity, darkness, death. It would be a living contradiction. Hence the struggle for holiness is also primarily a struggle for unity.

What the Christian does for unity in Christ is then the most decisive factor in his own sanctification. The greatest of all acts is to lay down one's life for the brethren, in union with the passion of Christ. It is the courage and uncompromising self-sacrifice of the martyrs, particularly of the bishop martyrs, that cements the unity of the Church in the fulfillment of the Eucharistic participation, in which the passion is represented by the union and solidarity of the faithful in love.

In brief: we respond to the call issued to us by Christ in His Passion. We come to unity in the Church, in obedience to the bishop, a unity from which no one can be excluded by reason of race, or social status. The more perfect this unity is, the more redolent it is of the odor of incorruption and immortality, the very presence of the Risen Christ. And this is witnessed by the joyous sacrifice of the martyrs.

4. *The Perfume of Incorruption*

The fact that St. Ignatius identifies holiness with "incorruption" shows that he is, in this and in everything else, profoundly realistic. His notion of holiness is first of all ontological. The holiness of the Christian is a participation in the life and holiness of God, through Christ. But since Christ is one with the Church, then holiness for the Christian consists in union with God through the Church. "It profits you therefore to continue your flawless unity that at all times you may have a share in God" (Ephesians 4:2).

Participation in the life and grace of Christ is described in very concrete terms by St. Ignatius. To share in the life and light of the Risen Savior is to share in His incorruption, and thus to have in oneself no part of death, of error, of hatred, of conflict. The sacred newness of life in Christ manifests itself through the unity of the faithful as a sublime "perfume of incorruption." Here we are reminded that Ignatius, like Gregory of Nyssa and Origen, is a true Oriental and that he loves the symbolic language of the "spiritual senses." Nor are they purely and simply symbolic to him. One feels that this "good odor of Christ" was something truly objective, that could be "perceived" by the baptized Christian. He says, in any case, that the presence of Christ in the unity of the faithful is as a "good odor of incorruption" while disunity and wrangling over suspicious doctrines makes the assembly "stink of corruption."

"The Lord permitted myrrh to be poured on His head that He might breathe incorruption upon the Church. Do not let yourselves be anointed with the malodorous doctrine of the Prince of this world" (Ephesians 17:1).

When they are united with the bishops and presbyters, the faithful present to the world a "pattern and lesson of incorruptibility" (Magnesians 6:2). What is this pattern and lesson? It is a revelation of the archetypal unity in the divine nature itself, the union of the Father with the Son. It is a manifestation of the inner mystery of God, through the unity of the Church in Christ. (See Ephesians 3 etc.) It is a manifestation of divine life in unifying charity, that overcomes all conflicts and establishes peace.

How important it is for us to remember this vital aspect of the doctrine of St. Ignatius and of the early Church. Wherever Ignatius speaks of "unity" we may substitute the word "peace." They are indeed the same thing. The power of Christ's victory is manifested in the way in which the Church brings peace and reconciliation to elements which, naturally speaking, cannot be reconciled. The divine and supernatural mission of the Church is above all a mission of peace. Hence it follows that the moral life of the Christian must be built solidly upon the foundation stone of unity and peace. The most important Christian virtues are those which contribute most to peace. These are above all charity, self-sacrificing humble submission, obedience, meekness, and of course at the root of all is that faith which keeps us in constant contact with Christ "our inseparable life."

When the faithful live thus in unity and peace, overcoming evil with good and disarming violence with meekness and submission to Christ, then they cannot help but be holy, for they are "steeped in God" (Magnesians 14:1). How can they be anything but incorruptible? How can they help filling the whole world with the perfume of incorruption?

It is in the light of this that we see the full meaning of St. Ignatius' famous description of the Eucharist as the "medicine of immortality." Not only does it in some mysterious way predispose the bodies of the Christians for a risen life in the new creation, after the parousia: but it is a medicine of immortality here and now, a source of incorruption, *precisely because it is the sacrament of unity* and of charity. It is the sacrament which deepens and matures our union with one another in Christ, which sanctifies us yet further, all together, in the one Christ. It is the sacrament by which the Church herself, one and holy, grows constantly in sanctity and incorruption. By uniting us more perfectly in the true Body of Christ, this sacrament therefore steeps us in His immortality, His purity, His incorruption.

"For my drink," cries Ignatius, "I want the Blood of Christ which is *incorruptible love*" (Romans 7:3). But this wine of incorruption leads to the noblest inebriation—that of martyrdom. For the martyr in laying down his life for Christ, the Church, attains to an incorruptible love, a love that is purely of God, unmixed by any appetite for the things of the world or of the flesh.

5. *Conclusion*

The beautiful image of "incorruption" communicating itself as a paradisiacal odor of new life was taken up and developed by many other Fathers of the Eastern Church. St. Cyril of Alexandria carries it further than Ignatius of Antioch and shows us, in so doing, that there was something incomplete about the ecclesiology of the martyr-bishop from Syria. Cyril says: "The Holy Spirit is like the perfume of God's essence, God's living perfume, a living and active perfume which brings the things of God to creatures and Himself assures them of a share in the substance that is above all that is" (*In Joannem* XI, 2).

Here we see, as in Ignatius, the mystery of our sharing in the divine life, the divine nature itself which is the supreme Holiness. We see too this sharing manifested as a mystical and life-giving perfume perceptible to the "spiritual senses." But Ignatius did not develop the idea that the Holy Spirit is our bond of union with the Father in Christ, as also the divine and sanctifying power of Love that reaches us from the mystery of the Godhead, in and through Christ.

The mystery of our sanctification in Christ is, then, that the love of God, the bond of the Father and the Son, the Holy Spirit, reaches out to us from within Christ, and brings to life divine love, the likeness of Christ in us. He makes Christ live in us when the love that comes to us from Christ becomes our love and remains in us while it also remains in Him. This same love, this same Spirit, unites us all to one another in Christ.

The doctrine of Ignatius is then, supremely simple and profound, full of rich implications. It is eminently realistic, in the sense that it flows from a divinely given experience of the inmost reality of the Mystery of Christ in His Church. The key to that experience is Ignatius' faith in the *reality* of the Body and Spirit of the Incarnate Word, the *reality* of the Passion and Resurrection of Christ, and the *reality* of our sacramental communion in His Body and Blood in those sublime liturgical mysteries where the members of Christ are "consummated in unity."

[1961]

35

TIME AND THE LITURGY

The Liturgy accepts our common, everyday experience of time: sunrise, noonday, sunset; spring, summer, autumn, winter. There is no reason for the Church in her prayer to do anything else "with time," for the obvious reason that the Church has no quarrel with time. The Church is not fighting against time. The Christian does not, or at any rate need not, consider time an enemy. Time is not doing him any harm, time is not standing between him and anything he desires. Time is not robbing him of anything he treasures.

To understand the attitude of the Christian and of the Liturgy towards time we must have a profound understanding of Christian hope and Christian trust. Fundamentally the Christian is at peace with time because he is at peace with God. He need no longer be fearful and distrustful of time, because now he understands that time is not being used by a hostile "fate" to determine his life in some sense which he himself can never know, and for which he cannot adequately be prepared. Time has now come to terms with man's freedom. When man is not free from sin, then time is his enemy because every moment is a threat of destruction: every moment may be the one in which the unreality which man has chosen, by sinning, is brought face to face with cataclysmic reproof and is shown to be the fruit of servility, the abnegation of freedom, the surrender to determination by forces lower than man.

But when man recovers, in Christ, the freedom of the Sons of God, he lives in time *without predetermination,* because grace will always protect his freedom against the tyranny of evil. The Christian then knows that time does not murmur an implicit threat of enslavement and final destruction. Time on the contrary gives scope for his freedom and his love. Time gives free play to gratitude and to that sacrifice of praise which is the full expression of the Christian's sonship in the Spirit. In other words time does not *limit* freedom, but gives it scope for its exercise and for choice. Time for the Christian is then the sphere of his spontaneity, a sacramental gift in which he can allow his freedom to deploy itself in joy, in the creative virtuosity of choice that is always blessed with the full consciousness that God wants His sons to be free, that He is glorified by their freedom. For God takes pleasure not in dictating predetermined solutions to providential riddles, but in giving man the opportunity to choose and create for himself solutions that are glorious in their very contingency.

Does this mean that all temporal acts and decisions are despised and abandoned to an inscrutable divine will while the Christian disports himself in a realm of disembodied, abstract and purely spiritual "freedom"? No, on the contrary, even the most humble and contingent decisions of earthly and temporal life come to participate in this Christian realm of praise.

Hence the Christian is not afraid of the clock, nor is he in cunning complicity with it. The Christian life is not really a "victory over time" because time is not and cannot be a real antagonist. Of course, the Christian life is a victory over death: but it is a victory which accepts death and accepts the lapse of time that inevitably leads to death. But it does this in a full consciousness that death is in no sense a "triumph of time." For the Christian, time is no longer the devourer of all things. Christian worship is at peace with time because the *lapse* of time no longer concerns the Christian whose life is "hidden with Christ in God."

The Liturgy also accepts the archetypal, natural image of a "sacred time," a primordial time which mysteriously recurs and is present in the very heart of secular time. Whenever the Gospel is sung in the Liturgy it begins with the formula "at that time" (*in illo tempore*) and the formula, in effect, destroys the passage of time, annuls all the time that has passed since "then," for in the Liturgy the "then" of the salvific actions of Christ is "now" in the redemptive mystery of the Church's prayer. Hence, though "at that time" may perhaps suggest something of the "once upon a time" of fairy tales, it is in reality a quite different dimension. It is not *out of time,* not an escape from the flux and fall of life, but an affirmation of the fulness of life, present "now" as it was "then," neither in time nor out of it. Change and duration are not set apart by the Church as absolutes in themselves. They are not the measure of realities with which she is concerned. Yet she uses our familiar experience of time as the "matter" so to speak of a sacramental and sanctifying action. Time is transformed by the Church's blessing and prayer.

History itself acquired a new meaning, or rather its hidden meaning was revealed, when the Word of God became incarnate and entered into history. Time itself was now an Epiphany of the Creator and of the Redeemer, the "Lord of Ages." And yet time also acquired a new solemnity, a new urgency, since the Lord Himself now declared that time would have an end.

We live in the kingdom of Christ, the new world, consecrated to God, the messianic kingdom, the new Jerusalem. The history of the kingdom is working itself out, but in the mystery of faith, hidden from the wise of this world (I Cor. 1:19–21) and the final day of its manifestation is reserved for the future—the end of time.

Time, which is now enclosed between the two advents of Christ—His first coming in humility and obscurity, and His second coming in majesty and power—has been claimed by God for His own. Time is to be sanctified like everything else, by the presence and the action of Christ.

The redemption is not simply a past historical fact with a juridical effect on individual souls. It is an ever present reality, living and efficacious, penetrating the inmost depths of our being by the word of salvation and the mystery of faith. The redemption is Christ Himself, "who of God is made to us wisdom and justice and sanctification and redemption" (I Cor. 1:30) living and sharing His divine life with His elect. To be redeemed is not merely to be absolved of guilt before God, it is also to live in Christ, to be born again of water and the Holy Spirit, to be in Him a new creature, to live in the Spirit.

To say that the redemption is an ever present spiritual reality is to say that Christ has laid hold upon time and sanctified it, giving it a sacramental character, making it an efficacious sign of our union with God in Him. So "time" is a medium which makes the fact of redemption present to all men.

Christ has given a special meaning and power to the cycle of the seasons, which of themselves are "good" and by their very nature have a capacity to signify our life in God: for the seasons express the rhythm of natural life. They are the systole and diastole of the natural life of our globe. Jesus has made this ebb and flow of light and darkness, activity and rest, birth and death, the sign of a higher life, a life which we live in Him, a life which knows no decline, and a day which does not fall into darkness. It is the "day of the Lord" which dawns for us anew each morning, the day of Easter, the "eighth day," the *Pascha Domini*, the day of eternity, shining upon us in time.

For fallen and unredeemed man, the cycle of seasons, the wheel of time itself, is only a spiritual prison. Each new spring brings a temporary hope. Autumn and winter destroy that hope with their ever returning reminder of death. For man living only in the flesh, only on the level of his nature, for man living without God, the great realities of human love and fertility are without issue. We are begotten by parents who disappear from the face of the earth and are forgotten. In our own turn, we grow, become strong, bring forth sons, and then we too fail, and die and are forgotten. Our sons in their turn will pass through the same cycle which ends inexorably in death, and in oblivion.

It is as if the whole of nature were striving upwards, but striving in vain. Generation after generation she kindles the flames of countless human spirits, capable of an eternal destiny, lives that have insatiable aspirations for love, for wisdom, for joy in God. The flames leap up for a brief moment then die down and are extinguished. They are followed by others. None of them can reach up into eternity. The cycle of the seasons reminds us, by this perpetual renewal and perpetual death, that death is the end of all. The universe which came into being will some day grow cold, perhaps, and die. What will remain? Such is the view of life and time implied by the Hellenistic mystery religions, with their ontological foundations in Platonism. Time, the realm of matter and of "becoming" is the prison of eternal and divine spirits who have been punished by their descent into bodies, and seek desperately some way to return to the pure spiritual realm which is their "home." This climate of dualism and myth has, in effect, influenced much Christian thought, though it is not found in the Bible.

The modern pagan, the child of technology or the "mass man," does not even enjoy the anguish of dualism or the comfort of myth. His anxieties are no longer born of eternal aspiration, though they are certainly rooted in a consciousness of death. "Mass man" is something more than fallen. He lives not only below the level of grace, but below the level of nature—below his own humanity. No longer in contact with the created world or with himself, out of touch with the reality of nature, he lives in the world of collective obsessions, the world of systems and fictions with which modern man has surrounded himself. In such a world, man's life is no longer even a seasonal cycle. It's a linear flight into nothingness, a flight from reality and from God, without purpose and without objective, except to keep moving, to keep from having to face reality. (See Max Picard: *The Flight from God*.)

To live in Christ we must first break away from this linear flight into nothingness and recover the rhythm and order of man's real nature. Before we can become gods we must first be men.

For man in Christ, the cycle of the seasons is something entirely new. It has become a *cycle of salvation*. The year is not just another year, it is the *year of the Lord*—a year in which the passage of time itself brings us not only the natural renewal of spring and the fruitfulness of an earthly summer, but also the spiritual and interior fruitfulness of grace. The life of the flesh which ebbs and flows like the seasons and tends always to its last decline is elevated and supplanted by a life of the spirit which knows no decrease, which always grows in those who live with Christ in the liturgical year. "For though the outward man is corrupted, yet the inward man is renewed day by day. . . . For we know if our earthly house of this habitation be dissolved that we have a building of God, a house not made with hands, eternal in heaven" (II Cor. 4:16; 5:1).

The Word of God having entered into time by His birth of a Virgin Mother, has changed the cycle of the seasons from an imprisonment to a liberation. The Church prays God, at Christmas, that "the new birth of Thy only begotten Son may set us free, whom the old bondage detains under the yoke of sin."

The liturgy makes the very passage of time sanctify our lives, for each new season renews an aspect of the great Mystery of Christ living and present in His Church. Each recurring season shows us some new way in which we live in Him, in which He acts in the world. Each new feast draws our attention to the great truth of His presence in the midst of us, and shows us a different aspect of the Paschal Mystery in our world, now in the temporal cycle, and again in His saints, now in His sacraments, and again in the hallowed building of His churches, in His altars, and in the relics of His saints.

The liturgical cycle renews our redemption in Christ, delivers us from the servitude of sin and from the corruption of a "fleshly" mode of being. The liturgical cycle shows us that though we are caught in a struggle between flesh and spirit, though we are indeed the "fighting Church"—the Church militant—yet the victory is already ours. We possess the grace of Christ, who alone can deliver us from the "body of this death." He who is in us is stronger than the world. He has "overcome the world." In the cycle of the holy year, the Church rhythmically breathes the life-giving atmosphere of the Spirit, and her bloodstream is cleansed of the elements of death. She lives in Christ, and with Him praises the Father.

And so, while the cycle of time is a prison without escape for the natural man, living "in the flesh," and doomed to disappear with all the rest of his world that passes away, and while time is for the man of our cities only a linear flight from God, for the believer who lives in Christ each new day renews his participation in the mystery of Christ. Each day is a new dawn of that *lumen Christi,* the light of Christ which knows no setting.

The liturgical year renews the mysteries of our redemption each day in the Mass and Divine Office. It renews our participation in particular mysteries of the life of Christ. It teaches us the ways of the saints and renews our union with them in the charity of the Spirit. It is a year of *salvation,* but also a year of *enlightenment* and of *transformation.*

The mysteries of the liturgical cycle not only bring new outpourings of the salvific waters of grace: they also enlighten our minds with insights into the ways of God, ever ancient and ever new. They teach us more of Christ, they show us more of the meaning of our life in Him, they make us grow in Him, they transform us in Him. Indeed, the liturgy is the great school of Christian living and the transforming force which reshapes our souls and our characters in the likeness of Christ.

Dom Odo Casel compared the liturgical year to a ring which the Church, the virgin bride of Christ, triumphantly displays as the sign of her union with the incarnate Word. This holy ring is the gift of Christ to His Church as a pledge of His love and of His fidelity to His promises. The "cycle" or "circle" of the liturgy, which eternally returns to its beginning, is a symbol of the unity of God who is eternally the same yet ever new.

More than that, however, the liturgical "ring" of feasts is a symbol of that first "cycle" of actions by which Christ redeemed the world—the "ring" created by His descent into time, His life, death, resurrection and ascension into heaven restoring all things, in Himself, to the Father.

"The Father Himself loveth you because you have loved Me and have believed that I came forth from the Father. I came forth from the Father and am come into the world: again, I leave the world and I go to the Father" (John 16:28).

These words of St. John show us that the Church's belief in Christ is not a mere static assent to His historical existence, but a dynamic participation in the great cycle of actions which manifest in the world the love of the Father for the ones He has called to union with Himself, in His beloved Son. It is not simply that we are "saved," and that the Father remits the debt contracted by our sins, but that we are *loved* by the Father, and loved by Him in so far as we believe that He has sent His Son, and has called Him back into heaven after having given all power into His hands.

In the liturgical year, the Church sees and acclaims this action of the Father who so loved the world that He gave His only begotten Son for the salvation of men. It is a dialogue between mankind and the Father, in which the Father manifests Himself in His Word, and in which the Church, filled with the Spirit of the Father and the Son, praises and magnifies the glory of the Father, together with the Son.

To enter into the liturgical cycle is to participate in the great work of redemption effected by the Son. "Liturgy" is "common work"—a sacred work in which the Church cooperates with the divine Redeemer in reliving His mysteries and applying their fruits to all mankind.

It is quite clear that the Church does not regard the liturgy as a mere source of aesthetic satisfaction, or as an expression of Christian culture which stimulates devotion and piety. Nor is it merely a way in which the Christian society becomes formally aware of its existence and its relationship to God, in order to praise Him. It is a *work* in which the Church collaborates with the divine Redeemer, renewing on her altars the sacred mysteries which are the life and salvation of man, uttering again the life-giving words that are capable of saving and transforming our souls, blessing again the sick and the possessed, and preaching His Gospel to the poor.

In the liturgy, then, the Church would have us realize that we meet the same Christ who went about everywhere doing good, and who is still present in the midst of us wherever two or three are gathered together in His name. And we meet Him by sharing in His life and His redemption. We meet Christ in order to *be* Christ and, with Him, save the world.

In order to understand the full meaning of the liturgy we have to grasp the liturgical conception of time.

The Christian "present" of the liturgy has something of the character of eternity, in which all reality is present at once. The past and the future are therefore made present in the mysteries of the liturgy. In the Advent mystery, the Church not only re-lives the longing of the prophets and the patriarchs for the Redeemer, not only prays to God for the grace of a "new nativity" at Christmas, but also anticipates the coming of Christ at the Last Day. In every liturgical mystery the Church embraces the whole history of man's salvation, while concentrating her attention, for the time being, on one particular moment of that history.

At Christmas, we celebrate the coming of God into the world. We look especially at His birth at Bethlehem and see how that birth reveals to us the infinite mercy of God. But at the same moment we return to the very beginning of all. The generation of the Word in the bosom of the Father is also present to us, and we go forward to the end of all when, having come again into the world at the Last Judgment, and taken all things to Himself, and made all things new, we ourselves will share, by glory, in His divine and eternal sonship and hear the voice of the Father saying to us, in Him: "This day have I begotten thee!"

In every liturgical mystery we have this telescoping of time and eternity, of the universal and the personal, what is common to all ages, what is above and beyond all time and place, and what is most particular and most immediate to our own time and place. Christ in His infinite greatness embraces all things, the divine and the human, the spiritual and the material, the old and the new, the great and the small, and in the liturgy He makes Himself all things to all men and becomes all in all.

The works which Christ accomplished in time remain in eternity, treasured in the Sacred Heart from which they came forth, and the liturgical mysteries make these works present to us each time they are celebrated. Not only that, the liturgy incorporates us in His mysteries and renews their effect in time and in space. By the liturgy, while remaining in time, we enter into the great celebration that takes place before the throne of the Lamb in heaven, in eternity. As the Church prays, "as often as this saving Victim is offered up, so often the work of our redemption is carried out" (Secret, ninth Sunday after Pentecost).

Liturgy respects the flow of time and of history and yet, because it is in the "fulness of time," it anticipates the final accomplishment of all that time means to the Church. Time is "baptized" and sanctified by the infusion of the divine light hidden in the liturgical mysteries, a light which flows forth to penetrate our living and our actions and to fill them with the presence of the Lord Christ, the *Kyrios Christos.*

In each new liturgical feast we celebrate Christ Himself, not just the various things which He did, or the exploits of His saints. At Christmas, we celebrate Christ, living and present to us in Mystery, and commune with the divine mercy that He manifests by His birth. At the Epiphany we celebrate Christ as present among us, diffusing upon the world the light and glory of the Father and making known the Father's plan for the salvation of the gentiles. At Septuagesima we return to the creation of the world, in the Word, who is present with us: we consider flight from God into the darkness of sin. We share with Christ the labors and sufferings of His public life in Lent; then we enter into His passion. In Holy Week, Christ is present in the midst of His Church as the Lamb slain before the beginning of the world, as the Servant of Yahweh whose sufferings were foretold by Isaias and Jeremias, as the Christ who is crucified even today in His holy Church. At Easter, He is present among us as risen and triumphant, and shedding upon us the light of eternal peace. At Pentecost He is present among us as the founder of His Church and the giver of the Paraclete Who manifests Him in His Church.

In all these liturgical seasons, as Dom Gueranger says, "Christ Himself is the source as well as the object of the liturgy. Hence the ecclesiastical year is neither more nor less than the manifestation of Jesus Christ in His mysteries, in the Church, and in the faithful soul. It is the divine cycle in which appear all the works of God, each in its turn . . . If every year the Church renews her youth as that of the eagle, she does so by means of the cycle of the liturgy; she is visited by her divine Spouse who supplies all her wants" (*Liturgical Year,* Vol. 1, 9–10).

Pope Pius XII canonized these teachings in the succinct formulas of *Mediator Dei*:

> Throughout the entire year, the Mass and the
> divine office center especially around the Person
> of Jesus Christ . . . When the sacred liturgy calls
> to mind the mysteries of Jesus Christ, it strives to
> make all believers take their part in them so that
> the divine Head of the Mystical Body may live in
> all the members with the fulness of His holiness.
> Let the souls of Christians be like altars on each of
> which a different phase of the Sacrifice of the High
> Priest comes to life again . . . Hence the liturgical
> year . . . is not a cold and lifeless representation of
> the events of the past, or a bare and simple record
> of a former age; it is rather *Christ Himself who is
> ever living in His Church.* (151, 152, 165)

But if Christ is "ever present" in the Liturgy of the Church, and if the Liturgical cycle is an "ever recurring" cycle of feasts, does this not imply a return to the old concept of cyclical time, the "myth of the eternal return"? Does this not re-establish us firmly in the ancient cycle of seasons, and does it not finally reduce the Christian liturgy to a glorified and spiritualized cult of natural fecundity and rebirth?

It is true that the myths and symbols of archaic worship have to some extent left their mark on Christian symbolism since the days when the Gospel was preached in the world of Greece and Rome. Nevertheless, all Christianity that is true to its origins preserves the purity and simplicity of that eschatological vision which makes time utterly transparent, for all time has now become "the time of the end."[1]

But in proportion as we regard our Christian life as the canonization of merely temporal and social patterns, and as we place our hopes in a Christianity fully rooted and established not in Christ Himself, regardless of time, but in time "with the approval of Christ," we will have an entirely different concept of Liturgy and of Christianity, we will make our worship the reflection and glorification of the institutional structures in which we imagine our temporal hope to be made secure.

Liturgical time loses its meaning when it becomes simply the complacent celebration of the *status quo,* and if the "present" of liturgy is merely the "given" situation in which we find our human security. The paradox of liturgical time is that it is humanly insecure, seeking its peace altogether outside the structures of all that is established, visible and familiar, in the hope of a Kingdom which is not seen. It is that hope and that alone that makes Christ present among us. Outside that eschatological hope there is no meaning and no dynamism in liturgical worship.

[1955]

The Sacrament of Advent in the Spirituality of St. Bernard

Advent is the "sacrament" of the PRESENCE of God in His world, in the Mystery of Christ at work in History through His Church, preparing in a hidden, obscure way for the final manifestation of His Kingdom. Monastic liturgy is generally worship of the Father in and through the *Risen Christ*, glorious in heaven, present to us on earth in His Spirit. The twelfth century Cistercians place a special emphasis on the coming of Christ by His Spirit to the Christian Person. Like the Rhenish mystics they contemplate His hidden birth in our lives, His Advent here and now in the mystery of prayer and providence. This is the special presence of God in the world that fascinates them and draws them to Him in meditation upon the Bible, where He is present in His Word and in the light generated by that Word in the heart of the Believer. This is their *devotio*.

1. *The importance of recognizing the coming of the Savior*

Vigilance is a particular expression of monastic purity of heart—the virginity of spirit "proper" to the life of contemplation. We have left all things to watch by night "on the walls of Jerusalem." We wait with lamps trimmed, like wise virgins, for the *Parousia*. This is a basic Christian truth, common to all, but especially emphasized by monks. It is a particularly important aspect of the spirituality of St. Bernard. *Vos nolo ignorare tempus visitationis.*[1]

In the prelude to the first Advent Sermon, St. Bernard contrasts the vigilant monk with those who pay no attention to the coming of the Savior. These are in no way aware that they need a Savior. Hence they are unaware of His presence. They are like those who perish in the deluge. Grasping at every straw, "as though for the roots of grass" they seek solidity only in what deceives them, because it can offer no support.[2]

It is for the monk to seek a reality that has real substance, and is not a mere appearance. The monk lives on the realities revealed by God to His Church, in the Bible above all. The way for the monk then to seize upon the substantial realities of life, those which are solid and permanent, is to enter with a *laudabilis curiositas* into the mysteries of faith in the liturgy of the Church. Following an austere and lonely path, deprived of earthly consolation, living in emptiness, aware of their dependence on God, Cistercians live "as little ones," the Children of the Church. In this way they seek God Himself, beyond all visible things, and because they seek Him in faith He comes to them hidden in the *Sacramentum* of Advent.[3] However, we must not think that this meeting with God is merely the result of denying the body and affirming the soul. It is the *whole man* who either goes out to meet Christ in His Advent, or rejects Him with indifference.

2. The Sacrament of Advent

Behind this expression of St. Bernard's we find something of the profound eschatology of St. Paul.

The *sacramentum* which St. Bernard finds in Advent is the *sacramentum*, the *mysterium* of which St. Paul writes to the Ephesians. It is the "sacrament" (or "mystery") of the divine will, according to the design which it pleased Him to form in Christ, to be realized in the fulness of time, *to unite all things in Christ*.[4] This mystery is the revelation of God Himself in His Incarnate Son. But it is not merely a manifestation of the Divine Perfections, it is the concrete plan of God for the salvation of men and the restoration of the whole world in Christ.

This plan is envisaged not as a future prospect but as a present *fact*. The "last things" are already present and realized in a hidden manner. The Kingdom of God is thus already "in the midst of us." But, the mystery can only be known by those who enter into it, who find their place in the Mystical Christ, and therefore find the mystery of Christ realized and fulfilled *in themselves*. For these, the Kingdom of God is mysteriously present. They not only enter the Church, or enter Christ, but Christ becomes their life (*mihi vivere Christus est*). They participate in the glory of the saints in light.[5] In a certain sense they become the "Church" since *they live entirely by the Church, and the Church lives in them*.[6]

Bernard sees that the Sacrament (of Advent) is the *Presence of Christ in the world* as Savior. In his theology Advent does not merely commemorate the Incarnation as a historical event, nor is it a mere devotional preparation for the Feast of Christmas, nor an anticipation of the Last Judgment. It is above all the "sacrament" of the Presence of God in the world and in time in His Incarnate Word, in His Kingdom, above all His presence in *our own* lives as *our* Savior. The sacrament of Advent is the *necessaria praesentia Christi*.[7] Here he repeats in more concrete and practical terms his statement of the necessity of our finding Christ the Savior here and now among us, that was brought out at the beginning of St. Bernard's First

Advent Sermon. Three reasons for our misery and helplessness:[8]

faciles sumus ad seducendum—we are deceived in our judgments of good and evil;

debiles ad operandum—our attempts to do good fail, lead to nothing;

fragiles ad resistendum—we do not succeed in our efforts to resist evil.

The presence of Christ in us overcomes these obstacles. By *faith* He dwells in our heart and shows us how to judge between good and evil. *Si enim ille in nos quis decipiet nos?* He cannot deceive or be deceived. He is the wisdom of God, always ready to teach us. Yet in order to have His light, we must use the grace He gives us to turn to Him in our difficulties. By *fortitude* He strengthens our weakness, so that we can do all things in Him. He never grows tired, for He is the power of God, ever ready to revive us and lift us up. But we must call upon Him for help in our battles. Finally, He "stands for" us, He resists within us. If He be for us, who is against us?[9]

The secret of spiritual fortitude is for us to abandon ourselves to Christ, the power of God, and then He Himself will overcome evil and deliver us from forces that we would never be capable of resisting by ourselves. This is the fortitude of faith.

Christ lives in the world in those who take Him for their light, their strength and their protection. It is for them that He came into the world in His Incarnation.[10]

3. *The Pascha Christi*[11]

Christ who is present in the world, living in His mystical body, His Kingdom, is also reigning in heaven. To enter into the Mystery of Advent is to enter into the *pascha Christi* or the passage of Christ through this world in order that He might raise up all creatures in Himself to heaven. Without actually using the expression *pascha Christi*, St. Bernard quotes Ephesians 4:9–10, about Christ Who descended into the "lower parts of the earth" in order to ascend again into heaven, "leading captivity captive," in order to fulfill all things.[12] Hence our life of grace is the life of the Risen Christ in us.[13] We are buried together with Him by baptism in death that as Christ is risen from the dead so also we may walk in newness of life.[14]

The Word was made flesh in the first Advent, entering into our world to pass through it (*pascha—transitus*), gathering the elect to Himself by the effects of His death and resurrection, in order that His Incarnation, prolonged in His Mystical Body the Church, might finally terminate in the glorification of the *Whole Christ* at the right hand of the Father in heaven.[15] For St. Bernard, as well as for St. John of the Cross,[16] the highest contemplation is a participation of the Mystery of Christ, the Mystery of the Cross, or what we have been calling the—*Pascha Christi*, the monk's obligation to live in heaven even while we are on earth.[17] Our life is hidden with Christ in God. St. Bernard quotes this text[18] to show that although Christ is present with us in this life which is therefore an anticipated heaven, in faith, nevertheless it is above all a heaven because He is reigning gloriously in heaven and pouring down upon us the grace of the Holy Spirit Who unites us in His risen life.

4. *It is easy for us to approach Him*

Our incorporation into the mystery of Christ, the gift of divine life, is a pure manifestation of God's charity towards us. In this is charity . . . *that He hath first loved us.* Etienne Gilson has shown the basic importance of this idea from St. John in the mystical theology of St. Bernard.[19] There were two reasons why we could not come to Him: we were blind and He dwells in inaccessible light. We were helpless, spiritually paralyzed, and He dwells infinitely far above us. We can never climb to Him, He must descend to us. This is most important in the mystery of Advent—God's descent to our lowliness out of pure love, not for any merit of our own. Divine mercy is most evident in the tenderness with which the infinite God tempers the strength of His light to the weakness of our eyes and becomes a Man like the rest of us.

> Our most gentle Savior and Physician of our souls descended from His great height and dimmed His brightness to suit our feeble eyes. He hid Himself in a lantern, as it were, taking upon Himself His glorious Body, most pure of every stain. This is the light and luminous cloud which the Prophet said He would ascend in order to come down into Egypt.[20]

We do not have to travel far to find Him. He is within us. This idea is also basically Pauline: "Do not say who will scale heaven for us?, as if we had to bring Christ down to earth or, Who will go down into the depth for us?, as if we had to bring Christ back from the dead. No, says the Scripture, the message is close to thy hand, it is on thy lips, it is in thy heart."[21] This is the "*verbum fidei*," the spoken word which plants the seed of faith in our hearts and introduces us into the Mystery of Christ or the *Pascha Christi*. It is by the word of faith, or the *verbum crucis*, that the "Advent" of Christ becomes a reality in our personal lives.[22] Above all this means "believing with the heart that God has raised Christ up from the dead." Such faith makes Christ live in our hearts[23] and opens the way to contemplation based on a charity which teaches us "to measure in all its length and breadth and height and depth the love of Christ, to know what surpasses knowledge."[24] Through charity the Holy Spirit works in our hearts "with a power that reaches our innermost being"[25] which makes us aware of the fact that we are the sons of God[26] and thus gives us a special knowledge of Him.[27] Its final effect is to transform us entirely in God. "The Spirit we have been speaking of is the Lord; and where the Lord's spirit is, there is freedom. It is given to us all alike to catch the glory of the Lord in a mirror with faces unveiled; and so we become transfigured into the same likeness, borrowing glory from that glory, as the spirit of the Lord enables us."[28] As St. Paul indicates, all this is preceded by metanoia, conversatio, a complete turning to the Lord, a conversion, which is nevertheless much more a coming of God to us: "I have answered thy prayer in a time of pardon, I have brought thee help in a day of salvation . . ."[29] Our task is to see that we do not "give God's grace an ineffectual welcome."[30] St. Bernard echoes these ideas: "It does not behove thee, O man, to cross the seas, to penetrate the clouds, or to cross the alps." (These thoughts were already expressed by St. Anthony of the desert in much the same terms.) St. Bernard continues: "No great journey is shown to you: if you wish to meet God, go as far as your own heart"—*Non grandis tibi ostenditur via*: USQUE AD TEMETIPSUM OCCURRE DEO TUO. Here he quotes Romans 10:8: *Prope est verbum in ore. . . .*

To find the word in our heart we must enter into ourselves not so much by *introspection* as by *compunction*. This is important. The inward movement of compunction is not so much a matter of hiding ourselves within ourselves, as a liberation of ourselves, which takes place in the depths of our being, and lets us *out* of ourselves from the inside. This liberation from concentration on ourself is the beginning of a conversion, a *metanoia*, a real inner transformation. By no means would St. Bernard have us lock ourselves up inside ourselves as we are, in order that we might remain that way. Nor does he even urge us to find a merely metaphysical presence of God in the depths of our being.

He is not thinking of something static, but rather of a dynamic work of God's power. We go to meet the transforming action of God in our souls. This spiritual encounter is an Advent, in which God comes to our inmost self and we find ourselves in Him. The meeting takes place in an act of living faith, and the first evidence of transformation is a liberation of ourselves in Christ manifested by *"oris confessio"*—confession of our faith.

It is quite clear that St. Bernard conceives this as a liberation, a breaking out of the prison of "selfhood." In particular it is a liberation from a miserable preoccupation with our own failings. *Saltem exeas de sterquilinio miserae conscientiae.* The true interior life is not our *own* life within the depths of our own being. It is the coming of God into our being, from which we have previously *gone out*, in order to make room for Him. God's presence, in His purity, gives us a true interior life, *puritas cordis*. He is of course the *"auctor puritatis."* By this "advent" He comes into the soul and enlightens it with His invisible presence.[31]

It is easy to come to Him because He comes to us in *mercy*, not in justice or in wisdom. (Christ, the "bee" nourished among the flowers of Nazareth, comes to us without a sting and with honey. *Ad nos veniens solum mel attulit et non aculeum, id est misericordiam et non judicium.*)[32] He comes as a physician to heal the wounds of sin.[33] He comes as a little one lest we be terrified; *Parvulus datus est parvulis ut magnus detur magnis.*[34] He is a lamb full of gentleness, Who, in order to take away all our fears, was born to His Virgin Mother without the pain of childbearing.[35]

Although He comes from afar, since He is infinitely above us in majesty, yet nevertheless He also comes from close at hand since He is ever with us as our Creator. Hence His Advent is less a *coming* than a *manifestation* of His presence, He being already there. *Non ergo venit qui aberat sed apparuit qui latebat.*[36]

5. *Advent and Judgment*

Although Christ does not come into the world to judge the world, the world is judged by its own response to the revelation of God's merciful love in the Incarnation. God has so loved the world that He gave His only begotten Son in order that everyone who believes in Him may not perish but have eternal life. He does not send His Son into the world to judge the world but in order that the world may be saved by Him.

Whoever believes in Him is not judged. But those who do not believe in Him are already judged.[37] On the eve of His Passion, as He is about to enter His "hour," Jesus cries out "Now is the judgment of the world." The word judgment in this context is an abyss of light and darkness. It seems to imply at the same time condemnation and salvation, rejection and justification. And indeed it is so, for the "world," in the sense of those who are opposed to Christ, judges itself and condemns itself by judging and condemning Him Who is the "light of the world."[38] But the "world" in the sense of those for whom Jesus is the Savior[39] is saved indeed by the judgment which puts the Redeemer to death and thus pays the price of ransom for the world's sins. Therefore Jesus immediately adds to the declaration that "Now the world is judged"—"Now the prince of this world is to be cast out" as a direct consequence of that "judgment." Thus in actual fact the judgment of the world is at the same time the salvation of those who receive Him and the condemnation of those who reject Him. Therefore St. Bernard says it is for us to enter into judgment within ourselves and make up our minds which side we are on.[40]

St. Bernard discusses this idea in a remarkably condensed and meaty passage on Achaz's refusal of the sign offered to him by God through the ministry of Isaias.[41] Achaz refuses to ask of God a sign, though he has been instructed to do so by God, through the prophet. Commenting on this disobedience, St. Bernard plays in counterpoint with Isaias, Job and Proverbs, St. Paul and the Gospel. It is a typical instance of St. Bernard's versatility in the use of Scripture. Bernard's sensitive ear could detect the Holy Ghost speaking simultaneously through the mouths of all the Sacred Writers, to give us the same message in different and contrasting forms.

The picture of Achaz blends with that of Herod. The words of Isaias become the words of Christ Himself. St. Paul provides a theological undertone of commentary on the dialogue of these telescoped figures.

"Isaias heard from the Lord: Go and tell that fox (Achaz) to ask a sign from the Lord in the depths. The fox has his hole (which is hell), but if he goes down into hell he will find Him Who traps the crafty man in his own wiles."[42] And again: "Go, says the Lord, and tell that bird to look for a sign in the heights above; but if he ascends into heaven there he will find Him Who resists the proud and tramples down with their own power the necks of the proud and the haughty." The allusions to St. Paul[43] recall the fact that in any case it is useless for man's pride to seek God by scaling the heavens, since He must come down to us—He must first love us.

Because Achaz refuses a sign of God's power (from on high) or of His wisdom (in the abyss), God nevertheless gives a sign of His *mercy* that those who were not terrified by His power or His wisdom, might be *attracted* by His love.[44]

And yet this "new sign" is simply a variation of the two all-embracing signs which had been offered to Achaz, for the charity of God reigning in Highest Heaven in Majesty brought Him down, in the form of a Servant, into the depths of hell for love of us, but only in order to gather us to Himself, to "restore all things in Christ" and raise us up with Him to the height of heaven. Here too, in this thicket of Scripture passages we find, as everywhere, the *pascha Christi* which is the Mystery and Sacrament of Advent.

Therefore, says St. Bernard, declaring the mystery and making manifest the meaning of the sign,

> God Himself will give you a sign in which His
> majesty and His charity shall be made known.
> Behold a Virgin shall conceive and bring forth
> a Son and His Name shall be called Emmanuel
> which means "God with us." Adam, do not run
> away! for God is with us! Fear not, O Man, nor
> tremble at hearing the name of God, for God is
> with us. He is with us in likeness of our carnal
> nature, He is with us in oneness. *Propter nos venit,*
> *tamquam unus ex nobis, similis nobis, passibilis.*[45]

To sum it all up, the very presence of God in the world in His Incarnate Son is the pledge of salvation to those who receive Him, but it is the condemnation of those who do not accept His mercy. This acceptance is a matter of awareness. They must know His majesty, they must meditate on His love.[46]

6. The three Advents

St. Bernard frequently returns to the idea of the "three Advents" of Christ. The first of these is the one in which He entered into the world, having received a Human Nature in the womb of the Blessed Virgin Mary. The third is the Advent which will bring Him into the world at the end of time to judge the living and the dead or rather, in the light of what has been said above, to make manifest the judgment which the indifferent have brought upon themselves by failure to receive His love and the salvation which the elect have accepted from the hands of His mercy.

The first Advent is that in which He comes to seek and to save that which was lost. The third is that in which He comes to take us to Himself.[47] The first is a promise and the third is its fulfillment. To meditate on these two Advents is to sleep between the arms of God with His left hand under our head and His right hand embracing us.[48] It is also to sleep "between the lots" (that is to say to "live at peace in the midst of our inheritance").

Meditation on the Mystery of the two Advents will be made fruitful by works of charity and will lead to our complete transformation in Christ. If we have lived our lives in imitation of His virtues and of His Passion, our spiritual transformation will lead eventually to a total transformation of our whole being, body and soul, at the resurrection of the dead[49] when "He will form this humbled body of ours anew, moulding it to the image of His glorified body."[50]

The three Advents of Christ are the fulfillment of the *Pascha Christi*. But so far we have only spoken explicitly of the first and third. The second is in a certain sense the most important for us. The "Second Advent" by which Christ is present in our souls now, depends on our present recognition of His *pascha* or *transitus,* the passage of Christ through our world, through *our own lives.*

Meditating on the past and future Advents, we learn to recognize the present Advent that is taking place at every moment of our own earthly life as wayfarers. We awaken to the fact that every moment of time is a moment of judgment, that Christ is passing by and that we are judged by our awareness of His passing. If we join Him and travel with Him to the Kingdom, the judgment becomes for us salvation. But if we neglect Him and let Him go by, our neglect is our condemnation! No wonder St. Bernard would not have us ignorant of the Second Advent, the "*medius Adventus,*" the "time of visitation."[51]

Meditation on the first Advent gives us hope of the promise offered us. The remembrance of the third reminds us to fear lest by our fault we fail to receive the fulfillment of that promise. The second Advent, the present, set in between these two terms, is therefore necessarily a time of anguish, a time of conflict between fear and joy. But this is a salutary struggle! It ends in salvation and victory because it purifies our whole being.[52]

Nevertheless, the middle Advent is more a time of consolation than of suffering if we reflect that here too Christ really comes to us, really gives Himself to us so that we already possess our heaven in hope.

> This middle Advent is the way by which we pass
> from the first to the third. In the first Christ was
> our Redemption, in the last He shall appear as
> our Life. In this present one, as we sleep between
> the lots (in our inheritance) *He is our rest and our*
> *consolation.*[53]

There is nothing inactive about this "sleep." It may mean quiescence, darkness and emptiness for our natural activity, no doubt. But in this "darkness" God comes to us and works mysteriously within us in spirit and in truth in order that the fruit of His work may be made manifest in the third Advent when He comes in glory and majesty.[54]

7. *The work of Christ in us in the "Middle Advent"*

Evidently, the work of Christ in us as "Lord of virtues" is to produce in us His own virtues, to transform us into Himself as we contemplate Him in the Mystery of Advent, imitating His humble, hidden and sacrificial life. The example of Christ then becomes an element in that "judgment" which is presented to us in the Sacrament of Advent. But are we to wait until we possess all His virtues before we can join Him in His passage through our lives? If that were the case we could never join Him. First of all, then, we must unite ourselves with His truth by our *humility*. If we judge ourselves in this present judgment in which the prince of this world is cast out, we are "judged perfectly," and can safely look forward to His coming as a Savior.[55]

The humility of Christ, living and efficacious in us, exalts us and unites us to Him in His glory. His humility makes us seek nothing in this world except to do perfectly the will of God. When we have this will of Christ in us, then the Father and the Son come to us and take up their abode with us even in the present life.[56]

Such is the hidden Advent in which wisdom, without noise of words, builds His house in our hearts, raising it upon seven pillars and turning our souls into His palace and His throne. The soul of the just man is the seat of wisdom, and therefore the work of our preparation is above all the work of justice.

St. Bernard describes this justice which makes us like unto God—it consists in giving everyone his due, our superiors, inferiors and equals—and even our body, for St. Bernard never condemns the body as such.[57] However, this work of "justice" must be crowned, as he told us above, by self-judgment which lays our soul open to the divine grace that "justifies" us by God's free gift. The first thing God asks of us is to judge ourselves, to recognize our nothingness, to keep ourselves convinced that we can do nothing without Him and that therefore we must receive all from Him. If we thus judge ourselves He will never judge us, because we will be full of His grace.[58]

The inner purity and humility, in which we learn to distrust our own powers and to depend on God for everything, without however neglecting any effort to do His will, gives us peace and joy even while we still labor as wayfarers in the journey toward the great eschatological meeting with Christ which will end history with the third and final Advent.[59]

8. *The Scriptures as "Advent"*

Our *viaticum* in the Church's journey from the first Advent to the third is the word of God. This should be quite obvious, since from the beginning we have been speaking of the "Mystery of Christ" or the "Sacrament of Advent" which is the Presence of Christ in the world, working out the divine plan to restore all things in Himself and bring them to His Father. Now this work of Christ is done in us by faith which expresses itself through charity.[60] But faith comes "through hearing" and "hearing" through the word of Christ.[61] Only in this way will everyone who calls upon the Name of the Lord be saved. For if they do not know His Name, how shall they call upon it?

It is all important to understand in what way the word of God, *sermo Dei*, enters into our lives to sanctify them and to nourish the Christ-life which is the "Sacrament" of His secret and personal Advent to each Christian.

St. Bernard once again quotes the Fourth Gospel: when we keep the word of God, God Himself dwells in us.[62] If God is to come into the secrecy of our hearts we must keep His word in that same inner sanctuary. *In corde meo abscondi eloquia tua!*[63] But what does it mean to keep these words in our heart? To remember them? To think about them? That is not enough. Indeed, to preserve the word of God in our minds as the object of speculation is to produce in ourselves the "science which puffeth up."[64] Besides, what is in the memory is easily wiped out by forgetfulness.

The material bread of this world, if it be kept in a cupboard, can be taken out by a thief or can grow mouldy there. Even so the word of God is useless to us, if it is merely "stored" in the mind or the memory. Just as we eat our material bread and nourish our bodies with it, so also we must "eat" the bread of life and feed our souls. To eat the word of God is first to absorb it into the depths of our being, by obedient and loving faith, then to let the power of the Word express itself in the vital activity proper to faith: in works of love, good habits, a perfect life. This then is what feeds and delights our life in the "second Advent."[65] When we are nourished by the word of God in Scripture, when we *live* the divine message of Biblical revelation, Christ gains possession of our entire being, drives out the last trace of the "old man" and manifests His presence in everything we do.[66]

Those who do not enter deeply into the Mystery of Christ, but who are content to skim the surface of their faith are not really nourished by the Sacrament of Advent. *Non omnes haec memoria pascit.*[67] The worldly minded man may "celebrate" the Mystery of Advent, but he does not rejoice in it. He does not abound in the rich interior life which comes from living the mystery. He merely goes through it as a matter of routine, *dies istos quadam arida consuetudine observantes!*[68]

However, St. Bernard readily admits that this contemplative penetration of the Mystery of Christ, this interior awareness which finds Christ veiled in the "sacrament" of Scripture, is not something that we can acquire merely by our own efforts. True, the words of scripture, which are "all full of the mysteries of heaven, demand a diligent reader who knows how to draw honey from the rock and oil from the hardest stone."[69] However, in the last analysis, this consoling illumination is always a gift of God, "dropping down dew from the heavens," so that our earth gives her fruit. The Sacred Writers themselves possessed the Holy Spirit. In some measure they communicate Him to us along with the words they wrote under His inspiration. However, God Himself must breathe in our hearts as we read the Scriptures. It is this divine action within us, enlightening us to receive Him in His revealed word, which is so to speak the *"res sacramenti"* of the Sacrament of Advent. The words in which St. Bernard invokes this divine action at the beginning of his Homilies on the *Missus est* provide a beautiful prayer to be used before a meditative reading of the Bible: *Utinam et nunc Deus emittat verbum suum et liquefaciet ea (aromata) nobis; fiant in cordibus nostris desiderabilia super aurum et lapidem pretiosum multum, fiant et dulciora super mel et favum.*[70] Freely translated:

> May God send forth His Word and may the Spices
> (of the inspired text) melt to give forth their
> fragrance; may the (meanings of the text) become
> more to us than gold or precious stone, and
> sweeter than honey and the honeycomb.

9. *Mary, the "Royal Way"*

One idea remains to complete St. Bernard's doctrine on the Sacrament of Advent. God willed that the Blessed Virgin Mary play a central part in the Mystery of the Incarnation and of our Redemption. He willed that the salvation of the world should depend on her consent.[71] Mary is the "royal way" by which the King of Glory descended into the world in order to restore fallen mankind to its destined place in heaven. *Virgo regia ipsa est via per quam Salvator advenit.*[72] If we leave her out of the Sacrament of Advent we shall never fully penetrate its mystery, since we need to go forth to meet our Savior on the same Road by which He came to us. *Studeamus et nos, dilectissimi, ad ipsum per eam ascendere, qui per ipsam ad nos descendit: per eam venire in gratiam ipsius qui per eam in nostram miseriam venit.*[73]

It would be out of place to quote at length the celebrated text of St. Bernard in praise of the Holy Name of Mary, words which the Church herself sings in the office of Matins for that Feast. Let it be sufficient to remind the reader that St. Bernard finds no trial and no difficulty in life that cannot be overcome by the invocation of Our Lady's Name. "Following her you do not go astray, praying to her you do not despair; thinking of her you do not err. With her upholding you do not fall, with her as guide you do not grow weary; with her as friend you reach your goal; thus you will experience in yourself how rightly it was said: The Virgin's name was Mary."[74] One of the key ideas in the Mystical Theology of St. Bernard is his summary of the whole work of Redemption in the phrase *Sapientia vincit malitiam*.[75] Man lost the taste, the experiential knowledge, of divine things (*sapida scientia*) in the fall. Adam's sin was primarily that form of pride which is so subtly analyzed by St. Bernard as *curiositas*.[76] Now in this work of reparation, divine Wisdom seeks to blot out every trace of evil. In order to do so most perfectly, it restores man to his former dignity in the same way in which he lost that dignity: through a woman. *Si via cecidit per feminam non erigitur nisi per feminam*.[77] It is through Mary that we are "reformed unto wisdom." It is over her that the Spirit of God broods, most lovingly in the accomplishment of His sublimest work, preparing to restore to man his lost taste for spiritual things by giving him, for his food, the Word Himself, incarnate, as the Fruit of this virginal flower.[78] From this text it is obvious that Mary is at the very heart of Cistercian mysticism. She is the Mother of our contemplation because she is the Mother of Jesus in us.

God, in this sublime work of His, operates without sound, without noise of words. The angel finds Mary praying in solitude, the door closed upon her, in secret. The beginning of the third Homily on the *Missus est* is a hymn in praise of Mary in Solitude, and it reminds us that even for the Cistercian cenobite, interior and even some degree of exterior solitude is necessary for contemplation.[79]

It is in the virginal silence and solitude of Mary's humble prayer that the Divine Word descends upon our earth as quiet as dew in the night. If it had not been for her solitude and her silence, our earth would have remained a desert indeed! *Vere sine ipsa non aliud quam terra arida sumus!*[80] Finding in her no obstacle to the word of His love, God pours out upon her the fulness of the Divine Bounty, the *pluvia voluntaria,* which takes possession of her without the noise of any human operation, *absque strepitu operationis humanae suo se quetissimo illapsu virgineum dimisit in uterum.*[81]

The Word comes into the world through the doors of Mary's silent and hidden prayer, and is then diffused through the whole world, as we receive Him from the Apostles who received Him from her; an apt commentary on St. Bernard's familiar teaching concerning the interaction of contemplation and apostolate in the life of the Church!

The main theme of the Homilies on the *Missus Est* is the idea that Mary is everywhere foreshadowed in Scripture. Since Jesus is the heart of the Scriptures and since He does not come to us except by Mary then, St. Bernard concludes, Mary is also the heart of Scripture. He reveals her to us in all the traditional types with which the liturgy makes us familiar. She is the "woman" who will crush the serpent's head. She is the valiant woman in the Proverbs. She if the bush that Moses saw burning in the desert without being consumed. She is the rod of Aaron, the shoot that springs from the stock of Jesse's ruined tree. She is Gedeon's fleece.[82]

In fact, for St. Bernard, all the Scriptures harmonize together like the instruments of a great orchestra, and through all these various instruments the One Spirit of God proclaims one message in different tones, all of them leading up to the final message of the angel to Mary herself in which the entire Old Testament finds its fulfillment. Mary is, in a sense, the Old Testament in herself. She gathers unto herself all the prophecies and all the miracles and reveals their meaning in giving birth to the Divine Word Who was contained and hidden in them.[83]

Present in all creatures by His power, present in reasonable beings as the object of knowledge, present in the saints by union of love, God now makes Himself present in the bosom of Mary in a totally new and extraordinary manner, united not only to her will but even to her flesh so that He Himself takes flesh of her substance. Jesus is at the same time the Son of God and the Son of Mary, *Et si nec totus de Deo nec totus de Virgine, totus tamen Dei et totus Virginis est.*[84]

This presence of God in Mary is itself the secret of Advent, the heart of the Mystery, for it is in Mary herself that the Son of God gave us the admirable *Sacrament* of Advent— *Filius tecum ad condendum in te mirabile Sacramentum!*[85]

[1952]

ADVENT:
HOPE OR DELUSION?

The certainty of Christian hope lies beyond passion and beyond knowledge. Therefore we must sometimes expect our hope to come in conflict with darkness, desperation and ignorance. Therefore, too, we must remember that Christian optimism is not a perpetual sense of euphoria, an indefectible comfort in whose presence neither anguish nor tragedy can possibly exist. We must not strive to maintain a climate of optimism by the mere *suppression* of tragic realities. Christian optimism lies in a hope of victory that transcends all tragedy: a victory in which we *pass beyond* tragedy to glory with Christ crucified and risen.

It is important to remember the deep, in some ways anguished seriousness of Advent, when the mendacious celebrations of our marketing culture so easily harmonize with our tendency to regard Christmas, consciously or otherwise, as a return to our own innocence and our own infancy. Advent should remind us that the "King Who is to Come" is more than a charming infant smiling (or if you prefer a dolorous spirituality, weeping) in the straw. There is certainly nothing wrong with the traditional family joys of Christmas,

71

nor need we be ashamed to find ourselves still able to anticipate them without too much ambivalence. After all, that in itself is no mean feat.

But the Church in preparing us for the birth of a "great prophet," a Savior and a King of Peace, has more in mind than seasonal cheer. The Advent mystery focuses the light of faith upon the very meaning of life, of history, of man, of the world and of our own being. In Advent we celebrate the coming and indeed the *presence* of Christ in our world. We witness to His presence even in the midst of all its inscrutable problems and tragedies. Our Advent faith is not an escape from the world to a misty realm of slogans and comforts which declare our problems to be unreal, our tragedies inexistent.

The Advent Gospels, like most of the other liturgical texts of the season, are sober to the point of austerity. Take for example the question of St. John the Baptist in Herod's prison, where he was about to undergo a tragic death that was at once cruel and senseless: "Are you He who is to come, or look we for another?" Strange and even scandalous words, which some have never been able to accept at their face value! How can John have meant such a question, when he had seen the Holy Spirit descending upon Jesus in the Jordan? Yet the directness with which the question was asked was the guarantee of its desperate seriousness: for at the close of his life, John was concerned not only, as we might say, for the "success of his mission" but more profoundly still, for the *truth of his own life, the truth of Israel,* indeed the *truth of Yahweh Himself.*

In our time, what is lacking is not so much the courage to ask this question as the courage to expect an answer. There are enough men, some of them great men, who think that the only authentic posture is the frank acceptance of hopelessness in the face of life. Perhaps one reason why Sartre takes this position is that he feels Christians are always giving themselves a cozy answer to a desperate question they do not have the courage to ask. In which case our glad acceptance of the answer may be something less than edifying.

St. Gregory the Great said that all Christians should continue the prophetic mission of John and point out the presence of Christ in the world. This may mean many different things. John was able to point out Christ at the Jordan, in a moment of fulfillment, which gave meaning to his whole life. But John also had to witness to Christ in prison, in face of death, in failure, when even the meaning of his other glorious moment seemed to have been cancelled out.

So too, we may at times be able to show the world Christ in moments when all can clearly discern in history, some confirmation of the Christian message. But the fact remains that our task is to seek and find Christ in our world as it is, and not as it *might be*. The fact that the world is other than it might be does not alter the truth that Christ is present in it and that His plan has been neither frustrated nor changed: indeed, all will be done according to His will. Our Advent is the celebration of this hope. What is uncertain is not the "coming" of Christ but our own reception of Him, our own response to Him, our own readiness and capacity to "go forth to meet Him." We must be willing to see Him and acclaim Him, as John did, even at the very moment when our whole life's work and all its meaning seem to collapse. Indeed, more formidable still, the Church herself may perhaps be called upon some day to point out the Victorious Redeemer and King of Ages amid the collapse of all that has been laboriously built up by the devotion of centuries and cultures that sincerely intended to be Christian.

The Advent of Christ in history is not essentially bound up with the development and progress of a Christian *civilization.* "Christendom" is, and has been a great thing, but it has never been an absolute and unqualified good or an end in itself. *Christendom* is not *Christianity.* It is not "the Kingdom" and it is not the Mystical Christ.

The reality of Christian culture certainly flows from the presence of Christ in the world, but it is not identical with that presence. Our Advent is, then, not a celebration of mere traditional cultural values, however great, however worthy of perpetuation. Advent is not a mere return, a recurrence, and a renewal of the old. It cannot be a return to childhood, whether personal or social. The coming of the Lord, which is the same as His "presence" is the coming of the new, not the renewal of the old, and Sacred History is like the Heraklitean river in which no man steps twice.

Yet, since the Kingdom is the "fullness of time" it does in some sense make the past present in its fulfillment. But the past fulfilled is not the past, it is not merely renewed, it is completely transformed into the present. Baptism is the fulfillment of the Exodus, not its commemoration. The Eucharist is the Sacrifice of the Lord made present in its eternal reality, not reenacted in a ritual drama which revives the past. These sacred realities have a kind of timelessness: not that they are static and eternal ideas, Platonic abstractions, but dynamic fulfillment of all that is temporal and incomplete. Thus they can at the same instant enter time and transcend it.

John's question: "Are you He who is to come?" contains a curious telescoping of time. The present merges with the future, and there is also a suggestion of the past, since it refers back to John's previous testimony that in Christ the Savior of the world had already come. Our own celebration of Advent contains this same curious telescoping of past, present and future. We not only believe that Christ "will come" but also that He "has come." And this focuses our attention upon the present in which, as far as human evidence is concerned, there may or may not be some visible sign of either.

Yet we believe that He who has come and will come is present here and now: that we are in His Kingdom. Not only that, but we *are* His Kingdom. And I think that explains why we are not always too happy about asking John's question, since it implies a questioning of ourselves, of our life, of our part in history, of the very meaning of the mystery of Christ in His Church. Surely, we believe that Christ is in us, that He lives and acts in the world because He is present in the

Church. And we are His Church. But what does this mean? Is this presence something "purely spiritual"? If it is so "spiritual" that it has absolutely no visible or meaningful effect in contemporary society, we might as well admit it has no meaning that our contemporaries are likely to be interested in. Shall we adopt this position, and write our contemporaries off as contumacious heathen ready for the flames of Gehenna? Or do they have a right to ask *of us* this perilous question: "Are *you* the Kingdom of Christ Who is come, the Prince of Peace, the Just One, the Messiah who comes to bring unity and peace to the divided world of man?"

Do they have a right to *see* in us some evidence of the presence and action of Christ, some visible manifestation of the *Pneuma*? Surely it is not impertinent of them to ask to be shown what we claim is present in us. And this claim is not a matter of esoteric and perilous theologies. Our favorite apologetic argument for the divine mission of Christ is the holiness of the Church. But how evident does holiness have to be? Where, with what frequency, and how incontestably does it have to be manifest? Is it sufficient that we should be the only ones to be aware that we are holy?

How shall we answer such questions or even dare to ask them, unless we understand the kenotic quality of the Advent mystery? The Christ who emptied Himself taking the form of a servant, dying on the Cross for us, brought us the plenitude of His gifts and of His salvation. But He continues in us a kenotic and hidden existence. The fullness of time is the time of His emptiness in us. The fullness of time is the time of our emptiness, which draws Christ down into our lives so that in us and through us He may bring the fullness of His truth to the world.

Here is where we must beware of our own biased concepts of "fullness" and of "fulfillment." It is true that the glory and the presence of Christ have sometimes visibly overflowed not only in spiritual charismata, but also in what one might call the charism of culture and the spiritual forms of *civiltà*. But obviously this "charism" is at best metaphorical or analogous, since it involves the "baptising" of forms that are very limited both in time and in geography. The more we are "full" with these fulfillments, and the more we identify the countenance of a prosperous culture with the face of the glorified *Kyrios*, the more we tend to be deceived by projection and wish-fulfillment, the greater the danger that our Christianity will become a vain "boast" in the sight of God. In such a case, the Advent of the Lord demands nothing more or less than a return to the "emptiness" of faith. It may even mean the destruction of the false image which we had set up in honor of our own achievement or which, set up in honor of the Lord, was yet not worthy of Him.

If the Lord wishes to live in us His self-emptying, His kenosis, it is not likely that He will tolerate in us the fullness and self-congratulation of collective arrogance. Upon whom will His Spirit rest but upon the humble and the poor? This does not mean that occasional or even widespread pride may validly cast doubts upon the truth of the Church: but it does mean that the strength and holiness of the Church are not, at that moment, where they are supposed and claimed to be. Indeed, it may happen that the best Christians are among those who think themselves for some reason or other bad Christians. This, too, may be part of the mystery of Advent, and it can remind us of Christ's way, as recorded in the Gospels: He came most readily and most willingly to those who had most need of Him, that is to the unfortunate, the sinful, the destitute—those who were "empty."

The Advent mystery is then a mystery of emptiness, of poverty, of limitation. It must be so. Otherwise it could not be a mystery of hope. The Advent mystery is a mystery of beginning: but it is also the mystery of an end. The fullness of time is the end of all that was not yet fullness. It is the completion of all that was still incomplete, all that was still partial. It is the fulfillment in oneness of all that was fragmentary.

The Advent mystery in our own lives is the beginning of the end of all, in us, that is not yet Christ. It is the beginning of the end of unreality. And that is surely a cause of joy! But unfortunately we cling to our unreality, we prefer the part to the whole, we continue to be fragments, we do not want to be "one man in Christ."

Theologically, since human nature was assumed by the Word of God in Christ, all humanity is at least potentially "the humanity of Christ" in the sense that every existing human nature belongs by right, and indeed in fact, to Christ. Hence the terrible truth that a mankind which belongs to Christ without perhaps knowing it, or without being able to really evaluate the meaning of so astonishing a mystery, is spiritually alienated from Him and is tearing itself to pieces.

The Body of Adam ("Man"), which should be the Body of God's Love, is torn with hate. The Body of Adam which should be transfigured with light, is a Body of obscurity and untruth. That which should be One in love is divided into millions of frenzied and murderous hostilities. Yet the fact remains: Christ the King of Peace has come into the world and saved it. He has saved Man, He has established His Kingdom, and His Kingdom is the Kingdom of Peace. Furthermore, *we* are His Kingdom. Yet we have devised a power capable of destroying not cities, not nations, but *Man*. "Are you He Who is to come, or look we for another?"

Christ, in answering John's disciples, gave them signs which, according to the preaching of the Old Testament prophets, were clear indication that the Messianic Kingdom had come. They were also indications that the "fullness of time" had come and that the old world had ended. These were the "last days," the days of fulfillment, the days of "the end" because they were days of the "beginning."

Advent for us means acceptance of this totally new beginning. It means a readiness to have eternity and time meet not only in Christ but *in us*, in Man, in our life, in our world, in our time. If we are to enter into the beginning of the new, we must accept the death of the old. The beginning, therefore, is the end. We must accept the end, before we can begin. Or rather, to be more faithful to the complexity of life, we must accept the end in the beginning, both together.

The secret of the Advent mystery is then the awareness that I begin where I end because Christ begins where I end. In more familiar terms: I live to Christ when I die to myself. I begin to live to Christ when I come to the "end" or to the "limit" of what divides me from my fellow man: when I am willing to step beyond this end, cross the frontier, become a stranger, enter into the wilderness which is not "myself," where I do not breathe the air or hear the familiar, comforting racket of my own city, where I am alone and defenseless in the desert of God.

The victory of Christ is by no means the victory of my city over "their" city. The exaltation of Christ is not the defeat and death of others in order that "my side" may be vindicated, that I may be proved "right." I must pass over, make the transition (*pascha*) from my end to my beginning, from my old life which has ended and which is now death to my new life which never was before and which now exists in Christ.

Christ's answer to the disciples of John was the answer of newness and of life: "Go and tell John what you have seen: the blind see, the lame walk, and the poor have the Gospel preached to them." Here are two kinds of eschatological signs, and they compenetrate one another, for they are all signs of life, proceeding from love. Evil ends, and gives place to good in a physical and visible way: blindness ends, sight begins. Sickness ends, health begins. Death ends, life begins. But all these signs are evidence of an inexhaustible living power, the action of Life Itself, bursting into time, defeating and reversing the work of time. Hence this power manifests the "fullness of time," in which time is no longer mere irreversible succession, mere passage from insufficiency to insufficiency. Above all, the raising of the dead is a reversal and a conquest of time: for normally when the "hour of death" has struck, there can never again be an "hour of life." Yet the "hour" of Christ, when it struck, was at once the hour of death, of victory, of life and of glory. "Father the hour has come, glorify your Son that your Son may glorify You."

More important than the eschatological sign of renewed physical life is the sign *par excellence*: "The Gospel is preached to the poor." This means that the prophetic message of salvation, the fulfillment of the divine promises is now formally announced to the *anawim*, to those who hungered and thirsted for the Kingdom because they had no hope but the Lord. And therefore the last days have come. It is the end, because the fulfillment which earth and time could not give, is now at hand. This fulfillment has begun because now Christ has appeared in the midst of the poor as one of them, and has taken them to Himself so that they are, in a most special way, Himself. What happens to them happens, in a very particular way, to Him (Matt. 25:37–45). (Cf. Matt. 5:3–6, 10, 11.) The Last Days have come not merely because the poor have *heard about* Christ but because they "are" Christ. The poor themselves now become an eschatological sign of Christ, a sign by which other men are judged, for "*if the wicked servant says in his heart: 'My Lord delays in coming' and begins to strike his fellow servants,* and eats and drinks with drunkards, the Lord of that servant will come on the day he does not expect and in the hour which he does not know, and will cut him off (from Man in Christ) and give him his portion with the hypocrites" (Matt. 24:48–50).

The mystery of Advent, therefore, centers in the fact that *God is now present in Man, and men will be judged according to their acceptance of this crucial truth,* in all its consequences. What we do to man, we do to Christ, the God-man. Hence the tragedy of contemporary disorders and injustice. It is not only that they prevent men from becoming one in Christ, but rather that they rend mankind in pieces when, in the Advent Mystery, Man already *is* at least inchoatively, one in Christ!

In the light of current events, this is a sobering if not a frightening doctrine. Who of us does not fail in this faith? But there is hope in St. Paul's famous text: Whether well or badly, we all build on one foundation, Christ Jesus. No other foundation stone can be laid down. We can build on this foundation with gold, or stone, or wood, or straw. In the Day of the Lord (the day, that is, of His "Advent"), each one's work will be tried by fire. "If any man's work remain, which he has built on the foundation, he will receive a reward. If a man's work burns, he suffers loss, He himself shall be saved: saved, however, as though by fire" (I Cor. 3:14–15).

This is the "tragic" aspect of the Advent mystery for sincere and faithful Christians. We do, indeed, love Christ. We are among those who, in St. Paul's phrase, "love His coming (Advent)" (2 Tim. 4:8). We work for Him, and for His Kingdom. But we are also blind, confused, weak, fallible. We have resisted, perhaps sometimes even extinguished His Spirit, and done so perhaps when we thought we were most zealous for His truth. There have been great mistakes. Heroic efforts have been sometimes made and wasted. When times of crisis come to shake us out of our complacency, this all becomes sadly evident. What then shall we say? Advent, in these sombre years of "wars and rumors of wars" reminds us that though our work may be judged, and found wanting, even totally consumed by fire, it is in the very fire that destroys our imperfect works that we ourselves can be saved

[1963]

THE NATIVITY KERYGMA

NOTE: Christianity is not so much a body of doctrine as the revelation of a mystery. A mystery is a divine action, something which God does in time in order to introduce men into the sanctuary of eternity. Being a religion of mysteries, Christianity is a religion of facts—divine facts, divine actions.

In celebrating the mysteries of Christ as they recur in time, the Church first of all announces these events: "Christ is born!" "Christ is risen!" She proclaims them, as a herald proclaims the triumphal entrance of a victorious King into a city. Her announcement, her proclamation of the divine event, is a work which she entrusts to her "heralds," her apostles, her preachers. Christianity is thus essentially kerygmatic: the priest is a herald, *kerux*, an angel of the Lord of Hosts, a voice crying out in the desert: "Make straight the ways of the Lord."

These pages are a proclamation, a *kerygma*, of the nativity of the Son of God, Our Lord and Savior Jesus Christ. They announce the fact of His birth. They proclaim the presence of His mystery among us *now*, this year. They say, as the Church also says in her liturgy, "This day, Christ is born, this day the Savior has appeared: this day the angels sing on earth and the archangels rejoice: this day the just exult, saying: Glory to God in the highest, alleluia."

Christ is born. He is born *to us*. And, He is born *today*. For Christmas is not merely a day like every other day. It is a day made holy and special by a sacred mystery. It is not merely another day in the weary round of time. Today, eternity enters into time, and time, sanctified, is caught up into eternity. Today, Christ, the Eternal Word of the Father, Who was in the beginning with the Father, in whom all things were made, by whom all things consist, enters into the world which He created in order to reclaim souls who had forgotten their identity. Therefore, the Church exults, as the angels come down to announce not merely an old thing which happened long ago, but a new thing which happens today. For, today, God the Father makes all things new, in His Divine Son, our Redeemer, according to His words: *ecce nova facio omnia.*

Therefore, the Church on earth joins with the Church in heaven to sing one same song, the new song, the *canticum novum* which the Prophet commanded all to sing after the world should have been redeemed by the Christ, Whose ancestor he knew, by revelation, that he should be. When David cried out: "Sing to the Lord a new song," he was the first precentor to intone the songs the Church would sing on this day in her liturgy, as she announces to the whole world salvation and joy. For, as Saint Leo says: "Today there has shone upon us a day of new redemption, a day restoring that which was long lost, a day of bliss unending."

So, with the *Alleluia* of victory, the triumphant cry of Easter on her lips, the Church renews the Paschal mystery in which death is conquered, the power of the devil is broken forever, and sins are forgiven: the mystery of the death and resurrection of the Savior who is born to us on this day. Today, the Church sings: *Dies sanctificatus illuxit nobis*, which means: A day of salvation, a day sanctified by mystery, a day full of divine and sanctifying power, has shone upon us. And she continues: "*Alleluia, Alleluia*: A sanctified day has shone upon us: come you gentiles and adore the Lord: for this day a great light has descended upon the earth." The Church summons all the world to adoration as she prepares with great solemnity to announce the words of the Gospel in her third Mass. This is the Prologue of John, in which with mighty power given him from God the greatest Evangelist proclaims that the Word, Who was in the beginning with God, is made flesh, and dwells among us full of grace and truth.

At Christmas, more than ever, it is fitting to remember that we have no other light but Christ, Who is born to us today. Let us reflect that He came down from heaven to be our light, and our life. He came, as He Himself assures us, to be our way, by which we may return to the Father. Christ gives us light today to know Him, in the Father and ourselves in Him, that, thus, knowing and possessing Christ, we may have life everlasting with Him in the Father. "For this is eternal life, that they may know Thee, Father, the one True God, and Jesus Christ, whom Thou has sent" and again, "As many as received Him He gave them the power to be made the sons of God."

Having realized, once again, Who it is that comes to us, and having remembered that He alone is our light let us open our eyes to the rising Sun, let us hasten to receive Him and let us come together to celebrate the great mystery of charity which is the sacrament of our salvation and of our union in Christ. Let us receive Christ that we may in all truth be "light in the Lord" and that Christ may shine not only *to* us, but *through* us, and that we may all burn together in the sweet light of His presence in the world: I mean His presence in us, for we are His Body and His Holy Church.

As Saint Paul says (and we sing this in one of the Epistles today): "In these days, God has spoken to us in His Son, Whom He has appointed heir of all things, by Whom also He made the world: Who being the brightness of His glory and the figure of His substance, and upholding all things by the word of His power, making purgation of sins, sits on the right hand of the majesty." And in another place the same Apostle says: "God who commanded the light to shine out of darkness has shined in our hearts, to give the light of the glory of God in the face of Christ Jesus."

Christ, light of light, is born today, and since He is born to us, He is born in us as light and therefore, we who believe are born today to new light. That is to say, our souls are born to new life and new grace by receiving Him who is the Truth. For Christ, invisible in His own nature, has become visible in our nature. What else can this mean, except that first He has become visible as man and second He has become visible in His Church? He wills to be visible in us, to live in us, work in us, and save us through His secret action in our own hearts and the hearts of our brothers. So, we must receive the light of the newborn Savior by faith, in order to manifest it by our witness in common praise and by the works of our charity towards one another.

These two things, this witness and this charity, are united together in the greatest of all our acts of worship in which we celebrate together the divine mysteries, thus proclaiming our faith, renewing our eternal covenant with God our Father, and receiving into our midst Him Who is the fountainhead of our faith as well as its object. We give Him, as it were, to one another, in the fraternal charity which unites us in the bonds of peace. For after Christ has been born in our hearts, He reaches out to Himself in the heart of our brother by the love of His own Spirit. Binding Himself, as He is in us, with Himself, as He is in our brother, He restores us, in that same Holy Spirit, to the embrace of the heavenly Father.

We are born today in Christ, to this embrace and to this peace. Can it be surprising that we feel in our hearts the exultation of the divine light which streams into our spirit from the presence of the newborn Savior and transforms us from glory to glory in His image?

This is the mystery of light which shines upon us today and which the Church everywhere proclaims in her sacred chants and texts. *Tu lumen, tu splendor Patris* she sings at Lauds, not only addressing Him Who is before her mystically, but also pouring forth the light and splendor of God that radiates from Him within her own heart. This splendor does indeed shine in the heart of every one of us who has received Baptism, the sacrament of light. It shines more brightly in all of us who have been inebriated with the fire of the Holy Spirit, and blinded by the glorious light from the most blessed Body of the Savior Whom we have received as our mystical nourishment. Indeed, the chalice of salvation has come to us overflowing with divine fire and the Body of the Lord has burned away the darkness and impurity of worldliness that kept us from seeing the One Who dwells in the midst of us, and Whom we know not: "Our God is a consuming fire." Therefore, in her various orations, the Church prays in the following words: "O God, Who hast made this most holy night to shine forth with the brightness of the true light, grant we beseech Thee that we may enjoy His happiness in heaven, the mystery of whose light we have known on earth . . . Grant that we who are bathed in the new light of Thy Word made flesh, may show forth in our actions that which by faith shines in our minds . . . Grant of Thy bountiful grace that through this sacred communion in mystery (*haec sacrosancta commercia*), we may be found conformed to Him in whom our substance is united to Thee . . . May our gifts, we beseech Thee, O Lord, be agreeable to the mysteries of this day's Nativity, and ever pour down upon us peace: that even as He Who was born Man shone forth also as God, so these earthly fruits may bestow upon us that which is divine."

In all these prayers, the Church plunges us into the Light of God shining in the darkness of the world, in order that we may be illuminated and transformed by the presence of the newborn Savior, and thus that He may be born and truly live in us by making all our thoughts and actions light in Himself. What joy, then, that He who dwells eternally in the inaccessible light and peace of the Father has left the throne of His glory and descended to be one of us! Or rather, without leaving the bosom of the Father, veiling the too brilliant light of His glory in the cloud of human nature, He who is enthroned above the cherubim takes up His abode among us in a poor manger. This Child whom the shepherds, dazzled by the brilliance of the angelic host, can scarcely see in the darkness of the cave lit by Joseph's lantern, this Child is (by His divinity) the Ancient of Days, the Creator and judge of Heaven and earth, of Whom the prophet Daniel wrote: "I beheld till thrones were placed and the Ancient of Days sat, His garment was as white as snow, and the hair of His head like clean wool; His throne like flames of fire: the wheels of it like a burning fire. A swift stream of fire issued forth before Him: thousands of thousands ministered to Him and ten thousand times a hundred thousand stood before Him." This, is Daniel's vision of the divinity of the Word Who, in His human nature, lies here helpless in the dark. But the Son of Man, who is here born, is Himself the Word, consubstantial with the Father. To this only-begotten Son, Who is equal to the Father in all things as God, but less than the Father in so far as He is man, all power is given by the Father. So, Daniel says again: "I beheld therefore in the vision of the night, and lo one like the Son of Man came with the clouds of heaven, and he came even to the Ancient of Days and they presented Him before Him, and He gave Him power and glory and a kingdom, and all peoples, tribes and tongues shall serve Him, His power is an everlasting power that shall not be taken away and His kingdom that shall not be destroyed." This, then, is the King promised from the beginning of the world and of whose Kingdom there shall be no end.

Do not be afraid of Him. God has emptied Himself and come to us as a child, in order that we who have not been saved by fear, but only destroyed by it, may now take heart and be saved by confidence. In "emptying Himself" and taking the form of a servant the Lord laid aside His majesty and His divine power, in order to dwell among us in goodness and mercy. Hear what the Fathers say: "The power of God had appeared before in the creation of the world, and His wisdom in the government of that which He had created: but the kindness of His mercy now appears most clearly of all in His humanity. He had made Himself known to the Jews in signs and wonders . . . But the Jews were crushed by His power and the philosophers who sought impudently to penetrate secrets of His majesty were blinded by His glory." These are the words of Saint Bernard. Neither power nor glory, then, can save us: for if the power and glory of God reveal themselves to our naked eye we will be blinded by their light and consumed by their fire. What then can be done? Saint Bernard cries, as the Church too cries out from age to age: "Let Thy goodness then appear, O Lord, that man, Who is created in Thy image, may be conformed to it." *Appareat Domine bonitas, cui possit homo qui ad imaginem tuam creatus est, conformari.*

We have seen that God has indeed answered this prayer, for all His goodness, all His love and all His mercy (which we were unable to see in the fearful storm upon Sinai or in the desert whirlwind), all the gentleness of the great God has appeared to us in Christ. *Apparuit benignitas et humanitas salvatoris nostri Dei!*

The Child that lies in the manger, helpless and abandoned to the love of His creatures, dependent entirely upon them to be fed, clothed and sustained, remains the Creator and Ruler of the universe. Yet, in this human nature of His, He wills to be helpless that we may take Him into our care. For here is no mere matter of appearances. The poverty of the Child and of His mother, their loneliness and dereliction at Bethlehem, their need for food and clothing and support, these are all as real as our own needs and our own limitations. And why? Above all, because of the reality of His love. He has embraced our poverty and our sorrow out of love for us, in order to give us His riches and His joy. He has become as poor as the poorest of us, that no man may be held back from Him by false shame. For, the love with which this divine Child loves us is truly the love of a man-child, but also, and just as truly, the love of our Savior and of our God. The arms with which He embraces us are not strong enough to harm any man, though they are the arms of God. What could be more evident than that God, Who loves us, and Who hates nothing that He has made, does not desire to hurt us? Can God will anything but our good? No, it is we who plunge to our own destruction by flying from His love.

Let us then, in the words of the Apostle, "deny ungodliness and worldly desires and live soberly, justly and godly in this world, looking for the blessed hope and coming of the great God and our Savior, Jesus Christ: Who gave Himself for us that He might redeem us from all iniquity and might cleanse to Himself a people acceptable, a pursuer of good works." But Saint Paul speaks here of another coming of the Lord, at the Last Judgment: for the Church would have us remember that without the consummation of Christ's work on earth, its beginning would have no meaning. The sacred Body which the Savior of the world took to Himself in the womb of the Virgin Mother has risen from death and reigns over heaven and earth, enthroned at the right hand of the Father. The Child whom we contemplate in mystery this day lives in fact in the bosom of the Father where He is ever begotten anew in the "day" of eternity, and where He governs the course of the world and of men's lives with omnipotent mercy. He Who is at once a Child and a King, and an Infant, and the Ancient of Days, looks with calm eyes upon the future day in which He shall give our flesh its share in His final victory over death. In that day, He who was once born to earth and time in a mortal Body will clothe our mortality with incorruption. "The trumpet shall sound and the dead shall rise again incorruptible and we shall be changed." For God became man in order that men might become gods.

If we wish to see Christ in His glory, we must recognize Him now in His humility. If we wish His light to shine on our darkness and His immortality to clothe our mortality, we must suffer with Him on earth in order to be crowned with Him in Paradise. If we desire His love to transform us from glory to glory into His perfect likeness, we must love one another as He has loved us, and we must take our places at that blessed table where He Himself becomes our food, setting before us the Living Bread, the Manna which is sent to us from heaven, this day, to be the Life of the World.

Jesus, Who has come to nourish our spirit with His own Body and Blood, does so not to be transformed into us, but in order to transform us into Himself. He has given Himself to us in order that we may belong to Him. For the center of this great mystery is the Eternal Father's design to reestablish all things in Christ. This, says Saint Paul, is the "Mystery of His will . . . in the dispensation of the fullness of times, to reestablish all things in Christ, that are in heaven and on earth."

This Child and Redeemer Who comes amid the songs of angels to answer the prayers of all the Patriarchs and Prophets, and to satisfy the unrecognized longings of the whole lineage of Adam, exiled from Paradise, comes also to quiet the groanings of all creation. For, the whole world has been in labor and in mourning since the fall of man. The whole created universe, with all its manifold beauty and splendor, has travailed in disorder longing for the birth of a Savior. "Every creature groaneth and travaileth in pain even until now . . . for the expectation of the creature waiteth for the revelation of the sons of God."

The Patriarchs and Prophets prayed for the coming of Christ in Bethlehem, and this first coming did not silence the groanings of creation. For, according to the words of the Apostle, which we have just heard, while man waited for the birth of Jesus in Judaea, the rest of the universe still waits for the revelation of Christ in His Church.

The mystery of Christmas therefore lays upon us all a debt and an obligation to the rest of men and to the whole created universe. We who have seen the light of Christ are obliged, by the greatness of the grace that has been given us, to make known the presence of the Savior to the ends of the earth. This we will do not only by preaching the glad tidings of His coming, but above all by revealing Him in our lives. Christ is born to us today, in order that He may appear to the whole world through us. This one day is the day of His birth, but every day of our mortal lives must be His manifestation, His divine Epiphany, in the world which He has created and redeemed.

[1956]

ASH WEDNESDAY

Even the darkest moments of the liturgy are filled with joy, and Ash Wednesday, the beginning of the lenten fast, is a day of happiness, a Christian feast. It cannot be otherwise, as it forms part of the great Easter cycle.

The Paschal Mystery is above all the mystery of life, in which the Church, by celebrating the death and resurrection of Christ, enters into the Kingdom of Life which He has established once for all by His definitive victory over sin and death. We must remember the original meaning of Lent, as the *ver sacrum*, the Church's "holy spring" in which the catechumens were prepared for their baptism, and public penitents were made ready by penance for their restoration to the sacramental life in a communion with the rest of the Church. Lent is then not a season of punishment so much as one of healing. There is joy in the salutary fasting and abstinence of the Christian who eats and drinks less in order that his mind may be more clear and receptive to receive the sacred nourishment of God's word, which the whole Church announces and meditates upon in each day's liturgy throughout Lent. The whole life and teaching of Christ pass before us, and Lent is a season of special reflexion and prayer, a forty-day retreat in which each Christian, to the extent that he is able, tries to follow Christ into the desert by prayer and fasting.

Some, monks and ascetics, will give themselves especially to fasting and vigils, silence and solitude in these days, and they will meditate more deeply on the word of God. But all the faithful should listen to the word as it is announced in the liturgy or in Bible services and respond to it according to their ability. In this way, for the whole Church, Lent will not be merely a season simply of a few formalized penitential practices, half understood and undertaken without interest, but a time of *metanoia,* the turning of all minds and hearts to God in preparation for the celebration of the Paschal Mystery in which some will for the first time receive the light of Christ, others will be restored to the communion of the faithful, and all will renew their baptismal consecration of their lives to God, in Christ.

The cross of ashes, traced upon the forehead of each Christian, is not only a reminder of death but inevitably (though tacitly) a pledge of resurrection. The ashes of a Christian are no longer mere ashes. The body of a Christian is a temple of the Holy Ghost, and though it is fated to see death, it will return again to life in glory. The cross, with which the ashes are traced upon us, is the sign of Christ's victory over death. The words "Remember man that thou art dust, and that to dust thou shalt return" are not to be taken as the quasi-form of a kind of "sacrament of death" (as if such a thing were possible). It might be good stoicism to receive a mere reminder of our condemnation to die, but it is not Christianity. The declaration that the body must fall temporarily into dust is a challenge to spiritual combat, that our burial may be "in Christ" and that we may rise with Him to "live unto God."

The ashes of this Wednesday are not merely a sign of death, but a promise of life to those who do penance. And yet the ashes are clearly a summons to penance, fasting and compunction.

Hence the seemingly paradoxical character of the Ash Wednesday liturgy. The gospel charges us to avoid outward signs of grief and, when we fast, to anoint our heads and to wash our faces. Yet we receive a smear of ashes on our heads. There must be grief in this day of joy. It is a day, we shall see, in which joy and grief go together hand in hand: for that is the meaning of compunction—a sorrow which pierces, which liberates, which gives hope and therefore joy. Compunction is a baptism of sorrow, in which the tears of the penitent are a psychological but also deeply religious purification, preparing and disposing him for the sacramental waters of baptism or for the sacrament of penance. Such sorrow brings joy because it is at once a mature acknowledgment of guilt and the acceptance of its full consequences: hence it implies a religious and moral adjustment to reality, the acceptance of one's actual condition, and the acceptance of reality is always a liberation from the burden of illusion which we strive to justify by our errors and our sins. Compunction is a necessary sorrow, but it is followed by joy and relief because it wins for us one of the greatest blessings: the light of truth and the grace of humility. The tears of the Christian penitent are real tears, but they bring joy.

Only the inner rending, the tearing of the heart, brings this joy. It lets out our sins, and lets in the clean air of God's spring, the sunlight of the days that advance toward Easter. Rending of the garments lets in nothing but the cold. The rending of heart which is spoken of in the lesson from Joel is that "tearing away" from ourselves and our *vetustas*—the "oldness" of the old man, wearied with the boredom and drudgery of an indifferent existence, that we may turn to God and taste His mercy, in the liberty of His sons.

When we turn to Him, what do we find? That "He is gracious and merciful, patient and rich of mercy." He even speaks to us in His own words, saying: "Behold I will send you corn and wine and oil and you shall be filled with them:

and I will no more make you a reproach among the nations."
This at the beginning of a forty days' fast!

It is necessary that at the beginning of this fast, the Lord
should show Himself to us in His mercy. The purpose of Lent
is not only expiation, to satisfy the divine justice, but above
all a preparation to rejoice in His love. And this preparation
consists in receiving the gift of His mercy—a gift which we
receive in so far as we open our hearts to it, casting out what
cannot remain in the same room with mercy.

Now one of the things we must cast out first of all is fear.
Fear narrows the little entrance of our heart. It shrinks up our
capacity to love. It freezes up our power to give ourselves. If
we were terrified of God as an inexorable judge, we would
not confidently await His mercy, or approach Him trustful-
ly in prayer. Our peace, our joy in Lent are a guarantee of
grace.

In laying upon us the light cross of ashes, the Church desires to take off our shoulders all other heavy burdens—the
crushing load of worry and obsessive guilt, the dead weight
of our own self-love. We should not take upon ourselves a
"burden" of penance and stagger into Lent as if we were At-
las, carrying the whole world on his shoulders.

Perhaps there is small likelihood of our doing so. But in
any case, penance is conceived by the Church less as a burden than as a liberation. It is only a burden to those who take
it up unwillingly. Love makes it light and happy. And that is
another reason why Ash Wednesday is filled with the lightness of love.

In some monastic communities, monks go up to receive
the ashes barefoot. Going barefoot is a joyous thing. It is good
to feel the floor or the earth under your feet. It is good when
the whole church is silent, filled with the hush of men walk-
ing without shoes. One wonders why we wear such things
as shoes anyway. Prayer is so much more meaningful without them. It would be good to take them off in church all the
time. But perhaps this might appear quixotic to those who

have forgotten such very elementary satisfactions. Someone might catch cold at the mere thought of it—so let's return to the liturgy.

To say there is joy in Ash Wednesday is not to empty the procession of its sorrows and anguish. "Save me O God," we cry at the very beginning, "for the waters are come in even unto my soul." This is not a song of joy. If we present our selves before God to receive ashes from the hand of the priest it is because we are convinced of our sinfulness.

That is a weak way of putting it. Sin is a thing that needs to be talked about in concrete and existential terms. A sinner, in the way the liturgy understands him, is not a man with a theoretical conviction that violation of the law brings punishment for guilt. A sinner is a drowning man, a sinking ship. The waters are bursting into him on all sides. He is falling apart under the pressure of the storm that has been breaking up his will, and now the waters rush into the hold and he is dragged down. They are closing over his head, and he cries out to God: "the waters are come in even unto my soul."

Ash Wednesday is for people who know what it means for their soul to be logged with these icy waters: all of us are such people, if only we can realize it.

There is confidence everywhere in Ash Wednesday, yet that does not mean unmixed and untroubled security. The confidence of the Christian is always a confidence in spite of darkness and risk, in the presence of peril, with every evidence of possible disaster. "Let us emend for the better in those things in which we have sinned through ignorance: lest suddenly overtaken by the day of death we seek space for repentance and are not able to find it."

The last words are sobering indeed. And note, it is the sins we have not been fully aware of that we must emend. Once again, Lent is not just a time for squaring conscious accounts: but for realizing what we had perhaps not seen before. The light of Lent is given us to help us with this realization.

Nevertheless, the liturgy of Ash Wednesday is not focussed on the sinfulness of the penitent but on the mercy of God. The question of sinfulness is raised precisely because this is a day of mercy, and the just do not need a Savior.

Nowhere will we find more tender expressions of the divine mercy than on this day. His mercy is kind. He looks upon us "according to the multitude of Thy tender mercies." In the introit we sing: "Thou hast mercy upon all (*Misereris omnium*), O Lord, and hatest none of the things which Thou hast made, overlooking the sins of men for the sake of repentance and sparing them, because Thou art the Lord our God."

How good are these words of Wisdom in a time when on all sides the Lord is thought by men to be a God who hates. Those who deny Him say they do so because evil in the world could be the work only of a God that hated the world.

But even those who profess to love Him regard Him too often as a furious Father, who seeks only to punish and to revenge Himself for the evil that is done "against Him"—One who cannot abide the slightest contradiction but will immediately mark it down for retribution, and will not let a farthing of the debt go unpaid.

This is not the God, the Father of our Lord Jesus Christ, who Himself "hides" our sins (*dissimulans peccata*) and gets them out of sight, like a mother making quick and efficient repairs on the soiled face of a child just before entering a house where he ought to appear clean. The blessings of the ashes know Him only as the "God who desires not the death of the sinner," "who is moved by humiliation and appeased by satisfaction." He is everywhere shown to us as "plenteous in mercy—*multum misericors.*"

And from the infinite treasure of His mercies He draws forth the gift of compunction. This is a sorrow without servile fear, which is all the more deep and tender as it receives pardon from the tranquil, calm love of the merciful Lord: a love which the Latin liturgy calls, in two untranslatable words, *serenissima pietas.* The God of Ash Wednesday is like a calm sea of mercy. In Him there is no anger.

This "hiding" of God's severity is not a subterfuge. It is a revelation of His true nature. He is not severe, and it is not theologically accurate to say that He becomes angry, that He is moved to hurt and to punish.

He is love. Love becomes severe only to those who make Him severe for themselves. Love is hard only to those who refuse Him. It is not, and cannot be, Love's will to be refused. Therefore it is not and cannot be Love's will to be severe and to punish.

But it is of the very nature of Love that His absence is sorrow and death and punishment. His severity flows not from His own nature but from the fact of our refusal. Those who refuse Him are severe to themselves, and immolate themselves to the bloodthirsty god of their own self-love.

It is from this idol that Love would deliver us. To such bitter servitude, Love would never condemn us.

This brings us to the meaning of the Lenten fast. It is not that food is evil, or that natural satisfactions are something God grudgingly allows us, preferring to deprive us of them when He can.

Fasting is a good thing because food itself is a good thing. But the good things of this world have this about them, that they are good in their season and not out of it. Food is good, but to be constantly eating is a bad thing and in fact it is not even pleasant. The man who gorges himself with food and drink enjoys his surfeiting much less than the fasting person enjoys his frugal collation.

Even the fast itself, in moderation and according to God's will, is a pleasant thing. There are healthy natural joys in self-restraint: joys of the spirit which shares its lightness even with the flesh. Happy is the man whose flesh does not burden his spirit but rests only lightly upon its arm, like a graceful companion.

That is why there is wisdom in fasting. The clear head and the light step of the one who is not overfed enable him to see his way and to travel through life with a wiser joy. There is even a profound natural rightness in this fast at the spring of the year.

These reasons are true as far as they go, but they are not in themselves a sufficient explanation of the Lenten fast. Fasting is not merely a natural and ethical discipline for the Christian. It is true that St. Paul evokes the classic comparison of the athlete in training, but the purpose of the Christian fast is not simply to tone up the system, to take off useless fat, and get the body as well as the soul in trim for Easter. The religious meaning of the Lenten fast is deeper than that. Our fasting is to be seen in the context of life and death, and St. Paul made clear that he brought his body into subjection not merely for the good of the soul, but that the whole man might not be "cast away." In other words the Christian fast is something essentially different from a philosophical and ethical discipline for the good of the mind. It has a part in the work of salvation, and therefore in the Paschal Mystery. The Christian must deny himself, whether by fasting or in some other way, in order to make clear his participation in the death of Christ. For the Paschal Mystery is the mystery of our burial with Christ in order to rise with Him to a new life. This cannot be merely a matter of "interior acts" and "good intentions." It is not supposed to be something purely "mental" and subjective. That is why fasting is proposed to the Christian by long tradition and by the Bible itself as a concrete way of expressing one's self-denial in imitation of Christ and in participation with His mysteries.

It is true that the present discipline of the Church, for serious reasons, has alleviated the obligation of fasting and in some areas has done away with it altogether. But certainly the Christian should desire, if he is able, to participate in this ancient Lenten observance which is so necessary for a genuine understanding of the meaning of the Paschal Mystery.

Finally, the ashes themselves are spiritual medicine, like all the sacramentals. The fruits of these apparently sterile ashes are wonderfully rich! Great is the secret power imparted to them by the influence of the risen body of Christ, who by His victory has become "life-giving Spirit."

The riches of this sacramental are clear from the prayers of the blessing. Blessed and sanctified by the sign of the cross, the ashes become a *"remedium salubre"* (health-giving medicine) and they bring *sanitas* (wholeness, cleanness) to the body as well as protection to the soul (*animae tutelam*), both of these availing for the remission of sins. They bring the grace of that humility which they signify, they bring also the pardon which we implore by the fact of receiving them.

They bring at the same time a realization of the horror of sin, and confidence of forgiveness. They bring with them all the aids necessary for the holy war of Lent, and they impart a special efficacy to our Lenten penances and prayers.

In a word, the ashes sign our whole being with the merciful blessing of God.

Armed with the grace of this great sacramental we begin a four-day preparation for Lent. For, as some may be surprised to learn, Ash Wednesday is not the beginning of Lent, but only the beginning of the Lenten fast.

The liturgical time of Lent begins on the following Sunday, and here the liturgy has a different character. It is more ancient and therefore more objective. The structure of the Sunday Mass is loftier and more noble in its splendidly simple architecture. Nothing is said about how a sinner feels, and the question of any possible conflict between the mercy and justice of God is not raised. All is bathed in the same pure light, the light of the wilderness where Christ the Lord fasts in solitude and is tempted by the devil.

The dramatic, medieval rites of Ash Wednesday may perhaps make a stronger and more immediate appeal to our feelings. The Mass of the first Sunday however leads us deeper into the real mystery of Lent, uniting us more profoundly and more directly with the Christ who, praying and fasting in us, will purify us and offer us together with Himself to the Father in the glory of His Easter victory.

[1958]

CHRISTIAN SELF-DENIAL

Jesus Christ, Who commanded His disciples to leave all things, take up their cross and follow Him, insisted that He was not of this world (John 8:23). The reason is clear. The "world," in this New Testament sense, refers to the society of those who would not and could not know the Living God. That is to say that although they might have conceptual knowledge about God and might indeed place Him at the center of their cosmic outlook and pay Him the respect of their worship, their life was such that it could in fact dispense with the "living and efficacious" intervention of His word. In fact their religion, their philosophy—or else their absence of either—was not a confession of dependence on God, still less a way of obedience to His commands, but a way of existence that justified itself by its implicit belief in man without God. This way of existence is the "way of the flesh," that is to say the way of obedience to the "will of the flesh" or man's will to self-assertion apart from God. An asceticism that fits into this context of "flesh" may indeed by very rigorous, extremely "spiritual." What marks it as "flesh" is its sustained appetite for a definitively self-achieved "perfection," independently of our condition of creaturehood. "For all that is in the world is concupiscence of the flesh and the concupiscence of the eyes and the pride of life which is not of the Father but is of this world" (I John 2:16). Jesus told His disciples that even the professionally pious, the Pharisees, whose lives were rigid and externally austere, had made themselves incapable of receiving His word and His Holy Spirit because they "judged according to the flesh" (John 8:15), and He added: "it is the Spirit that quickeneth. The flesh profiteth nothing" (John 6:64).

Now this Spirit of God is called by Jesus "the Spirit of Truth, which the world cannot receive; because it seeth him not nor knoweth him" (John 14:27). It is the Spirit of Truth that is opposed to the "will of the flesh." And here we must try to distinguish the Biblical concept of man from the Platonic view which has become almost inseparable from it in Western thought. The Bible does not divide man into a spiritual essence (soul) and an accidental body made of existence and neither of course does Orthodox Christian theology. Yet in the tradition of Christian Platonism, magnificent though it may be, Biblical anthropology has tended to take on a Greek coloring. The true life of man is said to be the life of the soul as *distinct from and opposed to* the life of the body. Christian asceticism comes to be seen as the liberation of the soul from a kind of "imprisonment" in the body. Temporal things, belonging to the realm of the body, are either evil or at best inferior to the spiritual things in the realm of the soul and of eternity. The "spiritual life" of man is then a withdrawal from time into eternity, and this in turn implies neglect of or contempt for the ordinary temporal active life of everyday. "Spirituality" then seems to demand the negation of everyday reality and a withdrawal into a realm of angels and pure essences, where eventually "union with God" will be attained outside time and beyond the contamination of all that is bodily and temporal.

Is this a genuinely Christian perspective? Is the function of self-denial merely to "liberate the soul" and withdraw it from temporal distractions and cares? Is not Christianity rather a humble and realistic acceptance of everyday life and of God's will in a spirit of obedience and liberty? Is not the true function of our self-denial the *clarification* of God's will in our regard, and the *unification* of our whole being, body and soul, in His service?

Those who are quickened to a divine life in Christ, by His Spirit, enter into intimate communion with the Truth. They possess the Truth. Truth lives in their entire being and manifests itself in all their activities, body and soul. The "Truth has made them free." Christ Himself is the Truth. And to achieve this union with Him, this freedom based on true values and firm adhesion to God's will, we must necessarily purge out of our hearts all attachment to false ego-centered values and all reliance on our own will. For there is no freedom in selfishness, only captivity. And there is no saving vision in the unaided intellect of fallen man. The limited truths he can still perceive seem to serve only to blind him, since in practice he never turns them to the one thing that matters, the glory of God.

Every page of the New Testament forces us to accept the conclusion which St. Paul expressed in such unequivocal language: "We are debtors not to the flesh (i.e., the ego-centered self), to live according to the flesh, for if you live according to the flesh you shall die, but if by the Spirit you mortify the deeds of the flesh, you shall live" (Romans 8:12–13).

There are still too many people who think that Christian abnegation means giving up all the best things in life in order to pay off a grudging debt to a severe Judge in Heaven, Who has a claim on us because we have sinned, and Who means to exact punishment by depriving us of a happiness to which we would otherwise be fully entitled. Even those who believe in a God of love are capable of making the same mistake, in a subtler and more roundabout way. God, they know, is a God of love. He wants us to be happy. But (and here is where the mistake comes in) they argue that therefore He cannot really want us to deny ourselves after all. You see, they, too, think that our happiness consists in the affirmation of the "flesh" in ego-centered satisfactions. They too, perhaps unconsciously, tend to base many of their practical decisions on what St. Paul calls the "wisdom of the flesh."

From the few lines of Scripture we have quoted, and from the text in which they are embedded, it is easy to see that far from making us unhappy, Christian self-denial is supposed to help us find perfect happiness by leading us rapidly to the fulfillment of our supernatural destiny. The principles on which St. John of the Cross bases his doctrine in the *Ascent of Mount Carmel* are doubtless rather strong meat. Nevertheless, those principles remain both clear and true. When the Spanish Carmelite says: "In order to arrive at having pleasure in everything, desire to have pleasure in nothing," he is teaching us the quickest way to happiness. The second half of his sentence is so bluntly stated that it may perhaps shock us into forgetting the first. But it is nevertheless true that the passions and desires of fallen human nature, because of their tendency to blind and weaken and exhaust the soul, constantly prevent us from fulfilling our highest capacities and therefore frustrate the need for happiness which is implanted in us all. It has been the constant and uninterrupted teaching of the Fathers and Doctors of the Church since the very first days of Christianity that a life without asceticism is a life of illusion, unreality, and unhappiness.

However, though it may be quite true that the genuine happiness of the human person is only attained when the self breaks out of its own narrow limits and is delivered from fixation upon its own satisfaction and affirmation, this is not the reason for Christian self-denial. There can be a genuine Christian *Eudaimonism*, or philosophy of happiness, and there is certainly such a thing as Christian humanism. An apologetic appeal to these values may be legitimate and may perhaps help to defend the Church against the accusation of remaining bogged down in Medievalism (as if there had been no happiness in the Middle Ages!). However, even if self-denial did not bring with it a certain satisfaction and an enlargement of our human capacities, it would still be necessary, because without it the Christian life cannot be fully centered on the essential obedience we owe to God, not only as our Creator but also as our Redeemer.

The call to "do penance" is based not on the fact that penance will keep us in trim, but on the fact that "the Kingdom of Heaven is at hand." Our penance—*metanoia*—is our response to the proclamation of the Gospel message, the *Kerygma* which announces our salvation if we will hear God and not harden our hearts. The function of penance and self-denial is then *contrition*, or the "breaking up" of that hardness of heart which prevents us from understanding God's command to love, and from obeying it effectively.

In order to do this we have to check and control all those impulses of that other "law in our members" which, as a matter of unpleasant practical fact, conflicts with the law of love and of grace. "The wisdom of the flesh is an enemy to God: for it is not subject to the law of God, neither can it be" (Romans 8:7).

However, no one can really embrace the Christian asceticism mapped out in the New Testament, unless he has some idea of the positive, constructive function of self-denial. The Holy Spirit never asks us to renounce anything without offering us something much higher and much more perfect in return. Self-chastisement for its own sake has no place in Christianity. The function of self-denial is to lead us to a positive increase of spiritual energy and life. The Christian dies, not merely in order to die but in order to live. And when he takes up his cross to follow Christ, the Christian realizes, or at least believes, that he is not going to die to anything but death. The Cross is the sign of Christ's victory over death. The Cross is the sign of life. It is the trellis upon which grows the Mystical Vine whose life is infinite joy and whose branches we are. If we want to share the life of that Vine we must grow on the same trellis and must suffer the same pruning. Even healthy shoots of natural life and energy, fruitful branches of our humanity, will have to be cut away. It is not only the evil that is in us that must be renounced. We are even asked to give up many good things: but only in order to get something better. "I am the true vine and my Father is the husbandman . . . every branch that beareth fruit, he will purge it, *that it may bring forth more fruit*" (John 15:1–2). It would scarcely be reasonable to suppose that the vintner attacks the vine with his clippers because he has a grudge against it, and wants to deprive it of its due.

There is no better or more complete source of ascetical theology than the Liturgy. Quite apart from the teaching in the Psalms and Bible texts, which are the actual word of God, the Church offers us in her collects and other prayers a most exhaustive and monumental theology of self-denial and supernatural living. To *live* the Mass that we all offer by active and intelligent participation is the normal expression of Christian metanoia.

Christian asceticism is remarkable above all for its balance, its sense of proportion. It does not overstress the negative side of the ascetic life, nor does it tend to flatter the ego by diminishing responsibilities or watering down the truth. It shows us clearly that while we can do nothing without grace, we must nevertheless co-operate with grace. It warns us that we must make an uncompromising break with the world and all that it stands for, but it keeps encouraging us to understand that our existence in "the world" and in time becomes fruitful and meaningful in proportion as we are able to assume spiritual and Christian responsibility for our life, our work, and even for the world we live in. Thus Christian asceticism does not provide a flight from the world, a refuge from the stress and distraction of manifold wickedness. It enables us to enter into the confusion of the world bearing something of the light of Truth in our hearts, and capable of exercising something of the mysterious, transforming power of the Cross, of love and of sacrifice.

But in that case, self-denial must mean something more than the triumph of our good self over our evil self, of reason over compulsion, or even more naively, of "soul" over "body." Actually it is not a question of resolving a conflict between two forces in ourselves but of submitting our whole being to the will of God in the "obedience of faith." This means much more than simply doing good and avoiding evil, much more than simply acquiring inner peace, and certainly more than just becoming thoroughly respectable and pious. It means entering into the Paschal Mystery of the death and resurrection of Christ by the total conversion of our entire self to Him by the Cross and a new life.

Liturgy is a ritual participation in the death of Christ (by which all our sins are expiated) and in His glorious Resurrection (by which His divine life is made our own) and in His Ascension (by which we enter with Him into heaven and sit at the right hand of the Father). We who offer the Holy Sacrifice and who receive into our hearts the Body and Blood of the Savior are building the Kingdom of Heaven on earth and in history. It is still a heaven possessed only in the darkness of faith and hope: yet the love by which Jesus unites us to Himself gives us a profound, sweet and experiential certitude of the union of our lives with His life and with one another in Him. We are already citizens of that Jerusalem that needs no sun and no moon because Christ is the lamp thereof. Here, for instance, is what a postcommunion, chosen at random in the Missal, tells us about the divine life we are already leading on earth. The Church addresses the Blessed Trinity in these words, after the people of God have received the Body and Blood of the Risen Savior: "Lord, may the action of this heavenly gift possess our minds and bodies so that our natural way of doing things may no longer prevail in us, but that the effects of this Communion may always dominate our lives" (15th Sunday after Pentecost).

Here we can see, first of all, that the Church clearly recognizes what her task is. God has placed in her hands divine instruments for our conversion and sanctification—the Sacraments. In fact, it is He Himself who, through the Church, works in our lives by means of these Sacraments. What is He doing in our lives? He is gradually taking over everything that we have and everything that we are, in order to gain complete possession of our souls, bodies and all our faculties, elevating them above the natural level and transforming them in His will. In other words, He is substituting His life for our life, His thoughts for our thoughts, His will for our will. This process of transformation leads to the end for which we were created—perfect union with God. It is only when we are perfectly united to Him that we become our true selves. It is only in Him that we can finally appreciate the true value of His creation. If he seems to deprive us of natural goods, we will find them all restored to us a hundredfold in Him.

Often in the course of the liturgical year the Church complains, in our behalf, that we are pressed down under the burden of our own human activity. That seems strange! To be free to do things in our own way would appear, at first sight, to be "the liberty of the sons of God." But no. As we enter into the ascetic life and advance in the ways of self-denial, we find that our biggest obstacle and our biggest burden is this old man of the sea, this body of death, this inescapable *self* we carry around with us. He is not our real self at all. He is the caricature of what we ought to be. But he rides us without mercy and, without the all-powerful help of God, we will never be able to shake him off. And he is the one who makes us act according to the "wisdom of the flesh." He is the father of all our worldliness. He is the one who prevents our liberation from "the world," and our transformation in Christ. He is the one who makes our life and work in the world a sterile and trivial assertion of our own futility.

And so we must remember that our asceticism is not directed against created things as such. Our real enemy is within our own castle. It is only because this enemy surrounds himself with the images and sensations and delights of created things and thus fortifies himself against all efforts of grace to dislodge him, that we must necessarily control our natural love for good things in order to fight him. When the Church prays, as she does, that God may give us the grace to despise earthly things and desire the things of heaven, she does not mean to imply that creation is evil: but that an ego-centered love of the good things of life is a source of darkness and evil in the world.

How does the liturgy look at created things? Everybody knows that the Church, realizing that all creation fell with Adam, intends to raise up all creation together with man, in the New Adam, Christ. It was in Christ that all things were made in the first place. "For in him were all things created in heaven and on earth . . . and he is before all and by him all things consist" (Colossians 1:16–17). To deliver creation from the power of evil, the Church has only to associate created things in man's worship of the Creator. Thus they begin once more to serve the purpose for which they were created—to lift man up, body and soul, to God. "For every creature of God is good, and nothing is to be rejected that is received with thanksgiving: *for it is sanctified by the word of God and prayer*" (I Timothy 4:4). Just take a glance at the liturgy of the Paschal Vigil at the *Exsultet* (where the bees come in for their measure of praise) and at the blessing of the font (where the Church becomes positively enthusiastic about water, calling it a "holy and innocent creature"). All this tells us what respect the Church has for God's creation. But the fact remains that she has no respect whatever either for the "world" or for the "flesh" and least of all for the devil. These three forces produce mental attitudes, ways of looking at things and doing things, which must be rooted clean out of the Christian life. Self-denial is then directed to this process of uprooting and liberation.

There are two extremes to be avoided. On one hand there is the error of those who believe that creation is evil and who therefore seek salvation and sanctity in an exaggerated asceticism that tries to sever the soul entirely from the rest of creation. This is the spiritual disease called "angelism." But on the other hand there is the error of those who act as if divine charity made no practical demands on human conduct: as if grace were merely a quality injected into our natural lives, making them automatically pleasing and meritorious in the sight of God, without any obligation on our part to live on the supernatural level of faith and Christian virtue. This attitude sometimes usurps the name of "humanism." Concerning those who cherish this view, the twelfth century Cistercian, St. Aelred of Rievaulx, wrote sardonically: "Although they do not say 'Let us eat, drink and be merry, for tomorrow we die' they say 'Let us eat, drink and be merry for we are full of charity!'"

True sanctity does not consist in trying to live without creatures. It consists in using the goods of life in order to do the will of God. It consists in using God's creation in such a way that everything we touch and see and use and love gives new glory to God. To be a saint means to pass through the world gathering fruits for heaven from every tree and reaping God's glory in every field. The saint is one who is in contact with God in every possible way, in every possible direction. He is united to God in the depths of his own being. He sees and touches God in everything and everyone around him. Everywhere he goes, the world rings and resounds (though silently) with the deep pure harmonies of God's glory.

But God cannot be glorified by anything that violates the order established by His wisdom. This order demands that man's body, and all that his body uses, be in subjection to his soul, and that man's soul be subject to God. Now this order is absolutely impossible, in our present state, without the generous and even severe practice of mortification. This order has been turned completely upside down by sin. The man who is outside the orbit of God's grace is not normally governed by reason but by passion. The mere possession of grace does not entirely deliver us from this state. It only puts in our hands the weapons by which we must win our freedom, helped by the power of God, through the merits of Christ's Cross, in His Holy Spirit. But the power of Calvary cannot avail in a life that does not in some measure enter into the mystery of Christ's Passion and death and Resurrection. "If any man will come after me, let him deny himself and take up his cross and follow me" (Matthew 16:24). "They that are Christ's have crucified their flesh with its vices and concupiscences" (Galatians 5:24).

We cannot use created things for the glory of God unless we are in control of ourselves. We cannot be in control of ourselves if we are under the power of the desires and appetites and passions of the flesh. We cannot give ourselves to God if we do not belong to ourselves. And we do not belong to ourselves if we belong to our own ego.

The real purpose of Christian asceticism is then not to liberate the soul from the desires and needs of the body, but to bring the whole man into complete submission to God's will as expressed in the concrete demands of life in all its existential reality. A spirituality that merely entrenched a man in the privacy of his own will and his own ego beyond the reach of all the claims of flesh, of history and of time, would not only be futile, but it might also confirm him in the evil of that spurious autonomy which is deaf to the call to salvation and obedience uttered in the Gospel Kerygma.

Self-denial is useless unless it opens the ears of our heart to obey the will of God commanding us to take our place in time, in history and in the work of building His Kingdom of Love and Truth. An asceticism that fails in this may actually strengthen our opposition and resistance to God by making us concentrate on our own autonomy and moral perfection instead of on the concrete obligation to love God and our fellow man.

St. Gregory Nazianzen speaks of the Christian as an "instrument played by the Holy Spirit." The aim of asceticism is to keep this instrument in tune. Mortification is not simply the progressive control of instinct by deadening the appetites of the heart. That is too crude a view. It is rather like the tightening of a violin string. We do not just go on twisting and twisting until the string breaks. That would not be sanctity, but insanity. No: what we must do is bring the strings of the delicate instrument, which is our whole being to the exact pitch which the Holy Spirit desires of us, in order that He may produce in us the exquisite melody of divine love that we were created to sing before the face of our heavenly Father.

False asceticism is not in tune with the Holy Ghost because it is a perversion of grace. And it is also a perversion of nature. It frustrates God's work and diminishes all our natural and supernatural capacities for good. The false ascetic is usually one who develops a kind of split personality. One half of his personality takes up arms against the other half and tries to destroy it. But this does not succeed. What happens then? The suppressed half of this unfortunate being withdraws into the "depths of the soul," and there healthy natural tendencies turn into unhealthy and vicious dispositions. That is why those who go about their self-denial in a crude and inhuman way are often proud, irritable and gross. That is why men who might have been saints have become fanatics, have persecuted the saints, and burned them at the stake.

Self-denial can assuredly bring peace to the soul that is troubled by all the cares, worries, sorrows and unrest that follow inevitably from attachment to created things. Asceticism roots out every plant from which the fruits of anxiety grow. The ascetic, then, should be a tranquil and happy man. His will be a simple and limpid soul, like a pool of clear water into which the sunlight of God's presence can enter without obstacle, to illumine and penetrate all. But this tranquility depends on the virtue of discretion. God demands that all Christians deny themselves but He does not ask the same kind of renunciation from a housewife with ten children as from a Cistercian monk—or vice versa! In the long run, it might well happen that the housewife might turn out to be more mortified than the monk: but she is not expected to do penance in exactly the same way. Her self-denial will be measured by the duties of her state as a wife and as a mother.

However, we must not imagine that the way of self-denial is always a way of tranquility and uninterrupted peace. It does not resolve all doubts and deliver us from every care as if by magic. Self-denial attunes us to the Spirit of God and the Spirit may not always sing a tune that harmonizes with our nature. There may be terrible discords instead of tranquil harmonies. Self-denial brings order into our lives sometimes in the form of an apparent disorder, and we may sometimes have to find peace as best we can in the midst of confusion. What matters is not the tranquility of our own heart but the sincerity of our faith and the totality of our obedience to God. But before we can begin to obey Him we must first recognize how profoundly inclined we are to disobey, and how difficult it really is for us to embrace a way of obedience to grace that means letting go of the security of our own self-hood and our own nature.

That is why the desire for ascetic works that pacify our minds and give us a sense of achievement may in fact prove to be an escape from the true and radical self-denial required of us by God.

Whatever may be the mode and measure of self-denial that God asks of us (and this is a matter that cannot really be decided without prayer and spiritual direction), all Christian asceticism is characterized by wholeness and by balance. Christ admits of no division. He who is not with Jesus is against Him. There is no fellowship between light and darkness, between the temple of God and idols. God asks us to give Him everything. But we have already said what that means: using all creatures for God alone. Consequently our asceticism must always be balanced. The true ascetic is not one who never relaxes, but one who relaxes at the right time and in the right measure, who orders his whole life, under the direct guidance of the Holy Spirit, so that he works when

God wants him to work, rests when God wants him to rest and prays constantly through it all by a simple and loving gaze that keeps his heart and mind united with the indwelling Spirit.

To such a one the Cross is always a source of strength and peace. "Because I am nailed to the Cross with Christ," says St. Thomas Aquinas, paraphrasing St. Paul and commenting on him, "because I am nailed to the Cross with Christ I have power to do good." Without the Cross, there is little spiritual vitality in our labors for God and His Church.

In a world in which there is so much involuntary suffering, it is not strange that there should be many men and women who begin to discover in themselves a totally unfamiliar desire to take upon themselves penances and mortifications for which there is no strict obligation. Wherever the Spirit of God works, He draws men away from the "wisdom of the flesh." Pleasures and achievements that once delighted their spirit now turn to ashes as soon as they are savored, and it becomes a pleasure for these Christians to do without the good things that most men have come to consider almost indispensable.

At the same time they become deeply aware of the radical insufficiency of arbitrarily chosen "ascetic practices" and of "methods" which are simply aimed at resolving moral conflicts within the self, and establishing the ego in a peaceful equilibrium. The true self-denial of the Christian is not a conquest of himself by himself, but a dying to self in order to live to God in Christ. This is the great question that preoccupied St. Paul—the problem of seeking salvation by the works of the law instead of by grace. Our salvation is not to be found in asceticism alone but in the Cross of Christ. Self-denial, however rigorous, lacks all Christian meaning apart from the Cross and Resurrection of Christ.

This is why Lent is a season of mortification and renouncement: not just because Christians discovered that a little fasting in Springtime was good for their constitutions, but because their fasts, renunciations and alms deeds had an essential part to play as signs of a full participation in the Easter Mystery.

The Church has relaxed the general laws of fasting in Lent, but this does not mean that Lent has now ceased to be a season of fasting and self-denial. It remains for the individual Christian, in the sincerity of his own conscience before God, to undertake such acts of self-denial and charity as will truly signify his will to die to himself and live in the Spirit of the Risen Christ.

[1950]

EASTER: THE NEW LIFE

Easter is not sufficiently well understood if we think of it only as the time when we reaffirm our belief that Christ rose from the dead. That the historical fact of the resurrection is the keystone of the whole structure of Christian faith is still not sufficient reason why Easter should be the great feast that it is.

Easter is not a day to be compared to the Fourth of July although it is in all truth the celebration of our Christian freedom. But this celebration does not merely recall the act by which we are liberated, it revives our freedom itself, in the renewal of the mystery in which we become free.

In any case, the Easter mystery is not celebrated only at Easter but every day in the year, because the Mass is the Paschal Mystery. Passiontide, Holy Week, Easter and the "holy fifty days" of the Easter season culminating in the celebration of Pentecost, all combine to spread the Easter mystery out before us in time in all its detail: but the fulness of Good Friday, Easter and Pentecost is also compressed within the compass of every day's Mass. For each time we participate in the sacred Mysteries, the *Pascha Domini* (The Passover of the Lord), we die with Christ, rise with Him and receive from

Him the Spirit of Promise who transforms us and unites us to the Father in and through the Son.

Lent has summoned us to change our hearts, to effect in ourselves the Christian *metanoia*. But at the same time Lent has reminded us perhaps all too clearly of our own power-lessness to change our lives in any way. Lent in the liturgical year plays the role of the Law, the pedagogue, who convinces us of sin and inflicts upon us the crushing evidence of our own nothingness. Hence it disquiets and sobers us, awakening in us perhaps some sense of that existential "dread" of the creature whose freedom suspends him over an abyss which may be an infinite meaninglessness, an unbounded despair. This is the fruit of that Law which judges our freedom together with its powerlessness to impose full meaning on our lives merely by conforming to a moral code. Is there nothing more than this?

But now the power of Easter has burst upon us with the resurrection of Christ. Now we find in ourselves a strength which is not our own, and which is freely given to us whenever we need it, raising us above the Law, giving us a new law which is hidden in Christ: the law of His merciful love for us. Now we no longer strive to be good because we have to, because it is a duty, but because our joy is to please Him who has given all His love to us! Now our life is full of meaning!

Easter is the hour of our own deliverance—from what? Precisely from Lent and from its hard Law which accuses and judges our infirmity. *We are no longer under the Law.* We are delivered from the harsh judgment!

Here is all the greatness and all the unimaginable splendor of the Easter mystery—here is the "grace" of Easter which we fail to lay hands on because we are afraid to understand its full meaning. To understand Easter and live it, we must renounce our dread of newness and of freedom!

Death exercises a twofold power in our lives: it holds us by sin, and it holds us by the Law. To die to death and live a new life in Christ we must die not only to sin *but also to the Law.*

Every Christian knows that he must die to sin. But the great truth that St. Paul exhausted himself to preach in season and out is a truth that we Christians have barely grasped, a truth that has got away from us, that constantly eludes us and has continued to do so for twenty centuries. We cannot get it into our heads what it means to be no longer slaves of the Law. And the reason is that we do not have the courage to face this truth which contains in itself the crucial challenge of our Christian faith, the great reality that makes Christianity different from every other religion.

In all other religions men seek justification, salvation, escape from "the wheel of birth and death" by ritual acts, or by religious observances, or by ascetic and contemplative techniques. These are means devised by men to enable them to liberate and justify *themselves.* All the other religions impose upon man rigid and complicated laws, subject him more or less completely to prescribed exterior forms, or to what St. Paul calls "elementary notions."

But Christianity is precisely a liberation from every rigid legal and religious system. This is asserted with such categorical force by St. Paul, that we cease to be Christians the moment our religion becomes slavery to "the Law" rather than a free personal adherence by loving faith, to the risen and living Christ; "Do you seek justification by the Law . . . you are fallen from grace . . . In fact, in Christ Jesus neither circumcision nor its absence is of any avail. What counts is faith that expresses itself in love" (Gal. 5:4, 6). And elsewhere he says that the only thing that matters for a Christian is his "new life"—the "new creature" which he has become in Christ (Gal. 6:15).

Hence the Christian has no Law but Christ. His "Law" is the new life itself which has been given to him in Christ. His Law is not written in books but in the depths of his own heart, not by the pen of man but by the finger of God. His duty is now not just to *obey* but to *live.* He does not have to save himself, he *is saved* by Christ. He must live to God in Christ, not only as one who seeks salvation but as one who *is saved.*

One might almost say that this truth is the great "scandal" of Christianity. It is the stone which is constantly being rejected by the builders. It is the element in our own faith which we fear and refuse to face, just as the Jews feared it and refused to face it in the challenge which Jesus flung at them by healing on the Sabbath, and calling Himself the "Lord of the Sabbath." Listen to St. Paul:

> Christ has set us free to enjoy freedom. Stand fast
> then and do not be caught again under the yoke
> of slavery . . . The Law has been our attendant . . .
> Since you have come to know God, or rather to be
> known by God, how is it that you turn back again
> to those weak and worthless and elementary
> notions and wish again to be enslaved to them?
> (Gal. 5:1; 3:24; 4:9)

Translated into our terms: Easter is the mystery of our redemption. We who have died and risen with Christ *are no longer sinners.* Sin is dead in us. The Law has no further hold on us.

And yet this is not as simple as it sounds. Our new life in Christ is not a permanent and guaranteed possession, handed over to our control, a "property" which we now definitively have. We are still suspended over the abyss, and we can still fall back into the awful dread of the alienated man who has lost trust. But the fact remains that *if we consent to it,* grace and trust are renewed from moment to moment in our lives. They are not a permanent possession but an ever present gift of God's love. For this liberty to continue, we must really believe in the power of God to sanctify us and keep us saints. *We must dare to be saints by the power of God.* We must dare to have a holy respect and reverence for ourselves, as we are redeemed and sanctified by the blood of Christ. We must have the courage to grasp the great power that has been given to us, at the same time realizing that this power is always made perfect in infirmity, and that it is not a "possession."

What about our own weaknesses? What about the law in our members, the law of sin and of death?

They are still there, but we do not have to dread them. We do not have to hate ourselves because their power still works in us. This power has been rendered harmless by the victory of Christ, as long as we remain firm in our faith, and trust in His power with a deep tranquil confidence. Thus we dare to live in the apparent contradiction that we are "sinners," still not immune to dread and loss of trust, and yet marvelously sustained by the presence and grace of Christ.

This trust means a delicate and loving subjection to the guidance of His Spirit, a careful and reverent attention to every indication of His will. We must dare to "feast in the unleavened bread of sincerity and truth"—that is to say, we must be perfectly frank (in so far as one can be frank) with ourselves, with our neighbor, and with God. We no longer have to conceal anything, because our past and even our present weaknesses are no longer a cause for shame. We do not have to excuse ourselves, justify ourselves. We have no longer any need for the bitter zeal which seeks to bolster up our confidence in our own virtue by seeking out flaws in the virtue of others. Such zeal is the old leaven of *those who are under the Law.*

We have not suddenly become angels. We have been sinners and can easily become sinners again. We are still "sinners," but ones who do not sin (I John 3:9). The fact remains that the most deadly influence in the life of the Christian is this spirit of slavery to the Law which frustrates the grace and liberty of Christ in our souls and disposes good and holy souls to fall back into sin. For that is precisely the function of the Law. "The Law intervened that the offense might become greater," said St. Paul (Rom. 5:20). The Law without Christ is a source of despair, whereas the cross of Christ and His Easter victory are our hope—our only hope—of real and total liberty from sin.

· Yet for some Christians, in practice, the cross has become the sign not of the victory of Christ, but of the victory of the Law. They look upon the cross chiefly as the sign of that punishment which is due to all who violate the Law. Such punishment was not due to Christ, they reason, but He took it upon Himself anyway, because of the great reverence due to the Law, and to show us how terrible a thing it is to break it.

Hence, in a strange, unconscious misunderstanding of the cross, we begin to act as if the cross were the greatest, most inescapable vindication of the Law. It is as if for us the blood of Christ had been shed not to deliver us from the Law by fulfilling it perfectly, once for all, in Himself. It is rather as if the blood of the Redeemer had been poured out in order to satiate and strengthen the Law forever, so that it could never die but would live on with the eternal sanction of a just God.

Both these aberrations are terrible in their falsity. Christ died on the cross, fulfilling the Law and thus becoming, for all those who are united to Him by loving faith, their complete fulfillment of the Law. "So, there is now no longer any condemnation against those who are in Christ Jesus. The norm of action of the spiritually minded which directs my life in Christ Jesus has delivered me from the inclination that entices me to sin and leads to death" (Rom. 8:1–2).

Nevertheless the Law remains the potential judge and adversary of each one of us, and it regains its grip on us as soon as we begin once more to live "according to the flesh," whether we do so by actual sin, or whether we merely substitute a fleshly and formalistic life of worship for the true eucharistic life in Christ.

The tenacious survival of the Law is no accident. It is intended by God, that the battle of Christ against the Law might continue in mankind until the end of time. It is necessary that this battle continue, and it continues in our own lives.

Why do we secretly keep cherishing a spirituality that is based on the Law rather than on Christ? Why do we fall back into dread, and fail to trust? Because it takes greater courage, more virile energy and more complete sacrifice of ourselves to embrace the liberty of Christ than to remain under slavery to the Law.

We can always evade this issue by confusing liberty with license and saying that in practice the two are indistinguishable. So that, according to this convenient theory, if one does not cling to the Law he will fall into license. There is no such thing for us as St. Augustine's "Love and do what you will!" We cannot call Augustine a heretic, of course, but we would certainly like to condemn this statement of his, and most of us seldom hesitate to do so with all the force of our outraged righteousness. Is this perhaps because we have a false notion of Christian liberty? Let us remember St. Anselm's doctrine that the "power to sin" is in fact not a power and has nothing to do with the true nature of freedom. He who is truly free is the one who has abandoned sin and renounced it so that, by God's grace, he is no longer inclined to choose evil.

We conveniently forget the real meaning of Augustine's aphorism. One who loves God, one for whom the love of God has replaced the "Law" as the guiding force of his life, does not want anything that is contrary to God's love. The moment he wilfully abandons the way of love and turns aside to will what is contrary to love, he loses his liberty, and falls once again under the tyranny of the Law.

And there, of course, he no longer can "do what he wills," he has to do what the Law prescribes, or else fall further under the deadly tyranny of sin. And the wages of sin is death.

Is the liberty of Christ then a scandal? Yes, frankly it is. It is too much for us, because we do not seriously consider plunging into a life of great apparent risks in order that we may be supported by the hidden power of God and guided by the Holy Spirit.

Indeed, this kind of thing has been viewed with the utmost suspicion. The risks are very real. Have there not been heresies that appealed presumptuously to grace? Have there not been great sinners who combined false mysticism with unbridled license under the pretext that they could love and do what they willed?

There have. But if we think that this is a reason for abandoning the liberty of the sons of God and putting ourselves once more under the Law, *we have emptied the Easter mystery of its most serious implications for our Christian life.*

Let us not therefore make the mistake of thinking that Christian perfection means binding ourselves tighter and tighter in a net of stricter and more minute prescriptions. The great sacrifices of the saints, their mortifications and their penances, so often misleading and misunderstood, were dictated not by Law but by the "spirit of life in Christ Jesus who had delivered them from the law of death" and their Christian greatness consists precisely in the fact that these acts were free, spontaneous and beyond any demand of Law.

It is for this reason that what is good for one saint is not good for another. What is a manifestation of liberty in one might be a sign of slavery in another. Those who consecrate themselves to God in the state of perfection should avoid all servile imitation of others in works that are of counsel, and which should proceed from our own spontaneous gift. The practices of others must never become for us a kind of law which we are bound to try to observe in fear. This is the secret of the shipwreck of many vocations.

Realization of this truth was perhaps what inspired some of the saints, like Francis of Assisi or Philip Neri, with acts of "holy folly" which remind us of the *yurodivetsvo*, the "folly for Christ," familiar in the spirituality of the Russian Church.

Those who keep the commandments of God in a spirit of servile fear, and thus make themselves "slaves of the Law," are often unconsciously striving to use the Law as cloak for the evil they feel in themselves. They try to observe the Law in such a way that the evil they do may not be imputed to them. And in this they subtly endeavor to turn the Law inside out, so that it becomes not their accuser but their defender.

But they cannot do this without tampering with the letter, stretching and distorting the meaning of the Law to make it cover their particular "cases." They do not realize that this manipulation of the letter turns the Law into a most deadly instrument. It is above all the legal-minded that "the letter killeth" at the very instant when they believe themselves to be saved by it.

Even when we are most sincere in our subjection to the Law, it remains a tyranny which is not willed for us by Christ, a tyranny from which He died to deliver us. Once again, let us turn to St. Paul and try to grasp the real meaning of our Christian liberty.

The most important thing that strikes us when we read the Pauline Epistles objectively, is that most of the things that many sincerely pious Christians worry about are things which do not matter:

> Let no one then call you to account for what you eat or drink, or for the observance of a festival or a new moon or a sabbath. These are but shadows of the realities which were to come, but the reality is Christ. . . . If you have died with Christ to the rudimentary notions which the world has to offer, why do you act as though you still belonged to the world by submitting to such rules as "Do not touch; do not taste; do not handle"! These are formulated according to merely human precepts and doctrines about things that perish in their very use. To be sure these rules have a show of wisdom with their self-imposed worship, their practices of humiliation and their unsparing treatment of the body, *but they are not to be held in esteem since they lead to the gratification of our lower nature.* (Col. 2:16–18, 20–23)

We must face the fact that the challenge of a passage like this is too much for many pious Christians. It is much too hot to handle. But if we are risen with Christ, if we are not "enemies of the cross of Christ," and if we believe in Christ's victory over the Law, we are going to have to understand works like these and put them into practice in our lives.

What is the trouble? Once again, it is this. We look at the Law as *the only possible alternative to sin.* There is the flesh, and there is the Law. Either you keep the Law, or the flesh carries you away. One or the other. It is better to keep the Law. Slavery to the Law is less degrading, less humiliating, and indeed it almost seems to endow us with a certain dignity. We are servants not just of the Law, but of God the Lawgiver. Unfortunately the cross and resurrection of Christ are there to make this evasion inexcusable.

If we look carefully at the famous contrast made by St. Paul between the "law of God in his mind" and "the law of sin in his body" we will see a little more in it than just these two.

It is true, St. Paul says he is "delighted with God's law according to the inner man," with his "mind he serves the law of God but with his lower nature the law which allures him to sin" (Rom. 7:22, 24, 25). Ordinarily this text is not interpreted fully. Very often for instance we take it to mean that there is nothing else for us but to accept this inevitable conflict, to try to keep the law of God in spite of the bias of concupiscence that draws us toward sin. To accept the conflict in a spirit of Christian resignation is all that is required of us as Christians.

Do we not see that this leaves us purely and simply captives of the Law? If this is all there is to it, then Christ's victory is not complete in our lives There is a third possibility, and this is the right one. It is the grace of God in Christ our Lord or, to be more succinct, *it is Christ Himself in us.* It is our new life in Christ. By our life of love and hope in Christ we rise above the dilemma and thus resolve it.

The Christian solution is not merely to continue struggling against temptation in order to live according to the Law. This is nothing new. It is exactly what had to be done before the coming of Christ. The Christian is no longer bound by the law of the flesh, and he is no longer obliged in a spirit of fear to keep the Law of God considered as a formal code imposed on him from without.

He may still be tempted by the flesh. He resists temptation and is saved not by various practices and stratagems but *by the spiritual force of love itself, and of the new life that is in him.* He lives by the "Spirit of him who raised Christ Jesus from the dead," and by that Spirit he "puts to death the deeds prompted by the animal instincts, and so lives" (Rom. 8:11, 13).

In other words, it is not dutiful observance that keeps us from sin, but something far greater: it is love. And this love is not something which we develop by our own powers alone. It is a sublime gift of the divine mercy, and the fact that we live in the realization of this mercy and this gift is the greatest source of growth for our love and for our holiness.

This gift, this mercy, this unbounded love of God for us has been lavished upon us as a result of Christ's victory. To taste this love is to share in His victory. To realize our freedom, to exult in our liberation from death, from sin and from the Law, is to sing the *Alleluia* which truly glorifies God in this world and in the world to come.

This joy in God, this freedom which raises us in faith and in hope above the bitter struggle that is the lot of man caught between the flesh and the Law, this is the new canticle in which we join with the blessed angels and the saints in praising God.

> God who is rich in mercy, was moved by the
> intense love with which he loved us, and when
> we were dead by reason of our transgressions, he
> made us live with the life of Christ . . . Together
> with Christ Jesus and in him he raised us up and
> enthroned us in the heavenly realm . . . It is by

grace that you have been saved through faith; it is
the gift of God, it is not the result of anything you
did, so that no one has any grounds for boasting.
(Eph. 2:4–9)

Let us not then darken the joy of Christ's victory by remaining in captivity and in darkness, but let us declare His power, by living as free men who have been called by Him out of darkness into his admirable light.

[1959]

A Homily on Light and
the Virgin Mary

*"No man lights a lamp and puts it under a bushel
basket."* Matthew 5:15

God our Father and Creator, Who is pure being, pure
truth, pure light, in Whom there is no darkness, willed to kindle the light of His truth outside Himself and for this reason
He made the universe.

The first of His material creatures was light, the purest
and most beautiful of all visible beings, from which comes
the beauty and the visibility of all other material creatures.
Light was a material image of His own truth and beauty. Yet
it was only the beginning of the work of God. It was not yet
the pure light of God Himself, shining mysteriously in a created being: it was only so to speak a shadow of God's light.

God, Who wished to kindle the lamp of His own truth,
fashioned the whole material creation as a lampstand for the
true light. We must always remember that matter is not a
bushel basket under which the light of God is hidden. Matter

is dark as long as it is without light: but it is not in itself a principle of darkness. It is capable of receiving light and truth in itself, and it can help to manifest them. Matter is dark only to those who seek no other light than matter itself. For them it is a source of darkness and of error. Now God made the lampstand, or the universe, by a word, commanding it to exist. But the lamp, man, He fashioned tenderly and carefully with His own hands.

As He made the lamp, He also breathed into it and kindled it with the light of His own truth, beauty and grace. For man, made in the image and likeness of God, shone with the very light of God within himself, he came into existence with divine light dwelling in his inmost being.

But as soon as the lamp was set on the lampstand, by an act of its own perverse choice, the lamp put out the light and refused to be rekindled.

Then there was a great darkness, even though the sun, moon and stars were all still shining where God had put them.

In the darkness, God continued patiently to prepare His true light: but now there was something in the lamp that had to be refashioned.

The lights which God kindled in the old Law were preparations for the perfect rekindling of the lamp: lights which were lit in worship and in justice, whenever man met God in liturgy, or in His works of mercy, justice and truth.

At first these lights were mysterious and quickly vanishing symbols like the rainbow shown in the covenant with Noah. Or they were frightening and inscrutable signs like the oven and torch shown in the covenant with Abraham:

> When the sun had gone down and it was dark,
> behold, a smoking oven and a flaming torch
> passed between the pieces. On that day the Lord
> made a covenant with Abram, saying, "To your
> descendants I give this land, from the river of
> Egypt to the great river, the river Euphrates."
> (Genesis 15:17–18)

Then at Sinai Yahweh set the whole mountain alight with a roaring fire hidden in cloud and thunder, which terrified the people:

> Now when all the people perceived the
> thunderings and the lightnings and the sound
> of the trumpet and the mountain smoking, the
> people were afraid and trembled; and they stood
> afar off, and said to Moses, "You speak to us, and
> we will hear; but let not God speak to us, lest we
> die." And Moses said to the people, "Do not fear;
> for God has come to prove you, and that the fear
> of him may be before your eyes, that you may not
> sin." And the people stood afar off, while Moses
> drew near to the thick cloud where God was.
> (Exodus 20:18–21)

And so it was seen that the light which God willed to kindle in man was too terrifying. Each time God approached the lamp, to light it again, the lamp was appalled and feared it would be destroyed. It fled from Him and hid in darkness. Then the Holy Spirit revealed a way of worship in which there were to be sacred lamps and lights, which would not terrify men but would yet speak to them gently of God's light. The lamps in the tabernacle were to be fed with "virgin oil," which would signify that virginal purity of heart which awaits the Bridegroom in the silence of night (Leviticus 24:1–4).

For the lamps of virgin oil, the inspired craftsman, the sacred artist Besalel made a lampstand, and perhaps he did not know, as he made it, that the Spirit in him was secretly refashioning an image of the universe, a cosmic paradise tree, in which man, under the form of innocent lamps, would shine again, full of the light of God, but as yet only in figure.

It is a curious thing that perhaps all man's work has in it something of this inescapable obsession—the desire to create a paradise around man, the desire to return to the beginning or to push on to an ideal consummation.

> The lampstand was made of pure beaten gold.
> The base and the shaft of the lampstand were
> made of hammered work; its cups, its capitals,
> and its flowers were of one piece with it. And
> there were six branches going out of its sides,
> three branches of the lampstand out of one side
> of it and three branches of the lampstand out of
> the other side of it; three cups made like almonds,
> each with capital and flower, on one branch, and
> three cups made like almonds, each with capital
> and flower on the other branch—so for the six
> branches going out of the lampstand. (Exodus
> 37:17–19)

These are significant words: for they tell us a truth about man's relation with the universe, and they instruct us about the importance of man's work as he lives in the world. Man, made in God's image, is placed in the paradise of the world, a world which is still paradise, but which man has lost, by becoming alienated from himself and from the Creator.

In this world from which he is alienated, man can come to find himself and recover his right relation to the world and to God, by the work which God has given him to do. Man's worship, his liturgy, should rightly be not only worship but a theology of life, a theology of work, planting in man the seeds of understanding and wisdom which will flower in his work. But this means that man's work must be purified of titanism, of self-will, of aspirations to self-assertion and power. And this means that it must be delivered from obsession with what man is not, with his past and future, what he has ceased to be and has not yet become, and is based on what man is in this present reality. For only in the present can man come in full contact with the truth willed for him and in him by God. Thus creation will become once again a lampstand, and man the lamp will be placed on it in order to be lit with the light of truth. For this is the light which God really intends to kindle in us. When we are in communion with other men and with the cosmos by our will, the light of truth is kindled in us.

The Book of Proverbs says: "The light of Yahweh is the spirit of man, penetrating to the depths of his being" (Proverbs 20:27).

When the spirit of a holy man is illuminated with the law of Yahweh, then the man himself becomes a light to his fellow man. So the prophets were lamps with which God "searched Jerusalem." David was said to be the "Lamp of Israel" (II Samuel 21:17).

On the one hand, when Yahweh wills to manifest Himself in His alienated creation, He does so in cloud, lightning and storm:

> He bowed the heavens, and came down; thick
> darkness was under his feet. He rode on a cherub,
> and flew; he was seen upon the wings of the
> wind. He made darkness around him his canopy,
> thick clouds, a gathering of water. Out of the
> brightness before him coals of fire flamed forth.
> The Lord thundered from heaven, and the Most
> High uttered his voice. And he sent out arrows,
> and scattered them; lightning, and routed them.
> When the channels of the sea were seen, the
> foundations of the world were laid bare, at the
> rebuke of the Lord, at the blast of the breath of his
> nostrils. (II Samuel 22:10–16)

Yet at the same time, while the storm rages outside in the world, the man who knows and trusts Yahweh, who sticks close to the Law of the Lord, perceives the Lord within himself as a lamp and a light to his feet:

> For thou art my lamp, O Lord, and my God
> lightens my darkness . . . God is my strong refuge,
> He makes my way blameless. (Id. 29, 33)

133

This text is familiar in the liturgy, where the Church applies it to Mary.

The Church celebrates, in Mary, the perfect rekindling of the pure light which had been extinguished by the sin of Adam. In Mary, the lamp was once more perfectly clean, burning with pure light, standing on the lampstand, illuminating the whole house of God, restoring meaning to all God's creatures, and showing the rest of men the way to return to the light: not that Mary was filled with any light of her own but because she was the first fruit of redemption, perfectly sanctified by the sacrifice of our redemption even before it was consummated, to give greater glory to the power of that sacrifice, and to prepare a way for the Lamb of God, the Light of the world, who was to come into the world through her consent and her obedience.

The liturgy applies to Mary the sublime texts from the Sapiential books about God's Wisdom itself. Since there is in Mary "nothing defiled," who is the "brightness of the eternal light and a mirror without stain. She is more beautiful than the sun, and compared with the light, she is found to be more pure than light itself."

How can these things be said of Mary? She is only a creature, and these words belong to the uncreated wisdom itself. But we must remember that the light that shines in Mary, the light that shone in Adam before his sin, and that God wished to shine in every man, is precisely the light of God's own wisdom, the reflection of His own truth, indeed His truth itself. For by the supreme liberality of God and the pure gift of His grace, man shares in the life, the light, the truth, the beauty of God and thus becomes the son of God in Christ.

No one has ever more perfectly contained the light of God than Mary who by the perfection of her purity and humility is, as it were, completely identified with truth like the clean window pane which vanishes entirely into the light which it transmits.

Mary is also described in the liturgy as the woman of the Apocalypse, "clothed with the sun with the moon beneath her feet, and with a crown of twelve stars about her head."

She is therefore filled with the light of the transfigured Christ, according to the words of the Gospel: her garments are "white as snow and her face is like the sun."

Thus she is "all beautiful," she is the "glory of Jerusalem and the joy of Israel." Indeed, the light that shines in Mary is the same light that is to shine in the whole Church and in the entire cosmos recapitulated in Christ. So, Mary is compared with the heavenly Jerusalem: "The Lord has shown us the heavenly Jerusalem filled with the light of God, and her light is like crystal and precious stone."

We who are sinners need the protection and light which comes from God. Without grace we cannot know the true light. Without His light we will go astray, and we will follow the false lights that our sin has kindled in the world. For as the Book of Proverbs tells us: "The light of the wicked is sin" (Proverbs 21:4).

Indeed, the world is hypnotized by strange and terrible lights, the fires that proceed from the mouth of Leviathan:

> His sneezings flash forth light, and his eyes are like the eyelids of the dawn. Out of his mouth go flaming torches; sparks of fire leap forth. Out of his nostrils comes forth smoke, as from a boiling pot and burning rushes. His breath kindles coals, and a flame comes forth from his mouth. In his neck abides strength, and terror dances before him. (Job 41:9–13)

This suggests to us the condition of our modern world in which, as Maritain has said, the great danger to society is the weakening of the sense of truth. The light that bursts from the mouth of Leviathan is not the light of truth but the flame of man's blind will to power.

For man today has lost consciousness of his need for truth. What he seeks is power. Truth is made to serve the ends of power. Truth is of no value unless it is expedient. When truth is not expedient, then it is deliberately manipulated and twisted to serve the aims of the powerful. Objective truth is considered irrelevant. It is derided by the powerful, who can change truth to suit themselves, and bend it this way and that for the sake of ambition and fortune.

It is a common trait of all the powerful materialist societies, that they are not so much interested in truth as in the creation and propagation of slogans and images. They specialize in thought-clichés, in glib formulas which made thought itself seem irrelevant. For to the man of power, thought is not expedient, especially in the subject whom he rules. What matters is will. Where power is primary, truth is made to bend to will. The will to power does not obey truth but manufactures its own truth, to suit policy and expediency. It imposes this fabrication ready-made on the subject to keep him from thinking for himself.

In such a condition, persons themselves become subservient to things. Indeed persons are treated as things. They are bought and sold like commodities. And therefore the rule of greed and fear replaces the rule of reason. Thought is regarded as a waste of time: all that matters is action for its own sake, action without reason and without ultimate purpose other than power.

But when power becomes more important than truth, when the affirmation of will becomes an end in itself to which all else is subordinated, then the whole purpose of the created universe is subverted and frustrated. The basic pattern of creation is this: material beings exist for man, and man exists for the glory of God. Created things stand as obstacles between man and God only when man himself is an obstacle, when his will has darkened the light of truth. But where the light of truth shines in man, and where he lives and acts according to that light, then all things find their proper place in relation to God by virtue of man's right use of them. They are sanctified and offered to God by man's creative work.

Thus everything else that has been created (except the angels) depends on man who is in the universe as the eye and the mind are in the body. If the eye is "single" or "simple," that is to say if it is pure, direct and true in its vision, then the whole body is full of light.

It follows then that the whole universe is in light or in darkness, spiritually, in proportion as man himself is in light or in darkness. If man's eye is "lightsome" with the spiritual beauty of grace, wisdom, understanding and divine sonship, then light will pass through him to pervade and transfigure the whole of creation: not of course by a kind of magical osmosis, but by the creative work of man's own spirit, a work born out of love for God the Creator and for our fellow man. Work that springs from this creative love is patterned on the truth implanted in our very being, by nature, and in our redeemed spirit by the Pneuma who is given us by the Risen Christ.

Man's obsession with power darkens and defiles the whole universe because it causes him to redefine all truth in terms of the power-struggle and to see all things in a partial, interested and fragmentary fashion. To define being in terms of power and will is to subject it to division and ultimately to atomize it. The uncontrolled obsession with will and appetite so divides and diminishes man that he cannot be whole, cannot be sane, and can never be at rest. But then he misuses and perverts everything he touches, and in the end all creation defies and frustrates him even while it obeys his supreme power.

As long as man seeks only to control the universe, he inevitably regards himself merely as a fragment of it. But the mystery of faith shows us he is indeed much more.

Man is more than a mere cog in a cosmic machine. Each person is in a way the end of the whole material creation which he transcends by his spiritual nature and by his vocation as a son of God. St. Thomas was saying this when he said that all the value of the natural world was less than the value of one degree of grace in the soul of redeemed man. He was also saying this when he declared that the rational soul of man is the last end intended for all lesser natures.

Only in Mary is this vocation perfectly realized. This explains why the liturgy shows her identified with the creative wisdom of God, as if she were so to speak what He intended before all else when He planned and fashioned the mountains, the stars and the oceans of the world.

> When He established the heavens I was there,
> when He marked out the vault over the face of
> the deep; when He made firm the skies above,
> when He fixed fast the foundations of the earth;
> when He set for the sea its limit, so that the waters
> should not transgress His command; then I was
> beside Him as His craftsman, and I was His
> delight day by day, playing before Him all the
> while, playing on the surface of the earth (and
> I found delight in the sons of men). (Proverbs
> 8:27–31)

In Mary is perfectly realized God's whole creative and redemptive plan. That is why she is said to be for us a light of truth and a pattern of life. That is why her spiritual beauty includes in itself all the beauty which we see here and there, in partial and incomplete form, in the universe. In her is all the beauty of the world, transfigured and elevated to a level beyond our comprehension: and yet since that perfection was reached by the fulfillment of the obediential potency in her nature, which is also our nature, there is a certain connaturality in us which makes us respond to her transcendent radiance even though it remains obscure to us. We cannot help but see that she is, like ourselves, a human creature whose littleness has been glorified in the light of Christ and who has been saved from the power of darkness and evil by the grace of His Cross.

It remains then for us to celebrate her immaculate beauty, to open our hearts to the same light of truth which sanctified her, the same grace which made her pleasing to the Most High, Who is her creator as He is ours, and who wishes to see realized in us the same ineffable mystery of light. More than that, He wishes to see the whole world saved and transfigured in that light, by reason of our perfect acceptance of His gift, His love and His grace and our transmission of the power of His love to all men and to all other beings by our work, our prayer and our love.

[1962]

THE GOOD SAMARITAN

"Who is my neighbor?"

Christ told the parable of the Good Samaritan in answer to that question.

To us, all Samaritans are "Good Samaritans." But it was not so to those who first heard the parable. In their eyes all Samaritans were, by the very fact, bad. Indeed that was why a Samaritan had to be the subject of the parable. It was necessary for the hearers to realize that at least one Samaritan could be a good one.

We on the other hand accept Samaritans without difficulty as good, having identified ourselves with them. All Samaritans are good in our eyes because we consider ourselves Samaritans—and good ones. Since we have come to regard ourselves as good Samaritans, do we not perhaps consider that Jews are less good than ourselves? In that case we will not understand the parable at all, for we shall imagine that the priest and Levite passes by the wounded man just because they were Jews. And we shall think that it was because the Samaritan was both "good" and "samaritan" that he helped him.

But if we interpret the parable in this way we close our minds to its meaning. For neither the Jew nor the Samaritan is our neighbor in any exclusive or comforting sense.

Consider the question that was asked: "Who is my neighbor?" This was, in fact, the second of two questions which a lawyer asked of Christ. His first, intended as a temptation or an embarrassment, was, "How shall I obtain eternal life?" This is an important question, and so important that nobody can be without the answer to it. And note that he asks this question of Him of Whom we read: "This is eternal life: to know Thee, the One True God, and Jesus Christ Whom Thou hast sent."

Since the answer to the most important of questions is accessible to everyone, the lawyer should have known it. And he did know it. He had no need to ask it at all. The Lord made this clear, for He said: "What is the first commandment?" When the lawyer replied, saying that the first commandment was the love of God and of our neighbor, then Christ told him to keep that commandment and he would have eternal life. In this way it became clear that the question was not necessary. But in order to prove that he had not asked it without reason the lawyer asked another question: "Who is my neighbor?"

We can perhaps assume that he meant by this to suggest that he had no problem about loving God, since "God is good," but that he was perplexed about loving his neighbor, since some men are better than others, and all are imperfect. This being the case, in order to protect himself against loving an unworthy object and thus wasting his love, he wanted to know where to draw the line. Who is the neighbor to be loved, who is the alien not to be loved? The question is a matter of rational classification. Therefore it is a matter of judgement also, for to classify is to judge. How then does one classify people, and judge them accurately as worthy of love, or of hatred, or of indifference? This is a pretty problem. But to the Lord it was a problem that had no meaning, for He said, "Judge not, that ye be not judged." Do not classify, and do not be classified.

The parable seems not to answer this question, or at least not to answer it directly. For the lawyer is saying, "How shall I identify my neighbor, in order actively to *give* him the love that is commanded by God?" and Christ gives an example of one who *needs* love, and who passively *receives* love from someone who falls outside the category of "neighbor." And yet the Samaritan is constituted a "neighbor" by the fact that he gives love. Now what this answer really says is more than the scribe explicitly asked. For the answer cuts right through the question.

Christ does not tell the scribe how to judge and classify, but teaches him that classifications are without significance in this matter of love. For we do not and cannot love according to classifications. Or if we do, then we do not love in the full sense of the word. Love is free, and does not need a good object: it can confer goodness that is hidden. But if love submits itself to an object, to a good outside itself, it tends to its own destruction. If it confers good upon its object, then it thrives and grows. For the nature of love is to give as well as to receive. It both gives and receives, but it gives first, and in giving it receives. Therefore if love demands first of all to receive a good from its object, before beginning to love, then it can never begin to love.

If a man has to be pleasing to me, comforting, reassuring, before I can love him, then I cannot truly love him. Not that love cannot console or reassure! But if I demand *first* to be reassured, I will never dare to begin loving. If a man has to be a Jew or a Christian before I can love him, then I cannot love him. If he has to be black or white before I can love him, then I cannot love him. If he has to belong to my political party or social group before I can love him, if he has to wear my kind of uniform, then my love is no longer love because it is not free: it is dictated by something outside itself. It is dominated by an appetite other than love. I love not the person but his classification, and in that event I love him not as a person but as a thing. I love his label which confirms me in attachment to my own label. But in that case I do not even love myself. I value myself not for what I am, but for my label, my classification. In this way I remain at the mercy of forces outside myself, and those who seem to me to be neighbors are indeed strangers for I am first of all a stranger to myself.

Do you think perhaps this is the meaning of the parable: that all men are to be loved because they are men? Because they are human, and have the same nature? No, this is not the meaning. That would be simply a matter of extending the classification to its broadest limits, and including all men in one big category, "Man." Christ however means more than this, for he gives a more than philosophical answer. His answer is a divine revelation, not a natural ethical principle. It is a revelation of the mystery of God. Hence in revealing truth, it remains mysterious and in some sense hidden. Yet if we get as close as we can to the source of revelation, we can gain deeper insight into the mystery.

The parable of the Good Samaritan is a revelation of God in a word that has great importance through all the Scriptures from the beginning to the end. It is a revelation of what the prophet Hosea says, speaking for the invisible God, "I will have *mercy* and not sacrifices." What is this *mercy* which we find spoken of everywhere in the Scriptures, and especially in the Psalms? The Vulgate rings with *misericordia* as though with a deep church bell. Mercy is the "burden" or the "bourdon," it is the bass bell and undersong of the whole Bible. But the Hebrew word which we render as mercy, *misericordia*, says more still than mercy.

Chesed (mercy) is also fidelity, it is also strength. It is the faithful, the indefectible mercy of God. It is ultimate and unfailing because it is the power that binds one person to another, in a covenant of wills. It is the power that binds us to God because He has promised us mercy and will never fail in His promise. For He cannot fail. It is the power and the mercy which are most characteristic of Him, which come nearer to the mystery into which we enter when all concepts darken and evade us.

There are other attributes of God which are further from Him and nearer to ourselves. They come and go in the Scriptures. They are flashes and presences, they appear and disappear as if they were in some sense provisional, as if they were approximations: they are too partial. All concepts of God have to be corrected and completed in so far as they are analogies. Some however more than others. For example the metaphor that He is angry, when in fact He is not angry. It is true that He manifests His wrath, that He judges, He punishes and He "strikes"! But when we say that He does all these things, He does not do them but something else which we do not understand. And when it has been said that He is angry it has only been said that it seemed to us that He was angry. We are saying that if we had been in His place we would have been angry and would have struck. But because "my thoughts are not your thoughts, says the Lord," there is something much nearer the truth which appears on a transcendent level when the anger vanishes. This is the sun which does not change, behind the passing clouds which are other attributes of God. This unchanging, fundamental, stable element is the mystery which is revealed in the Hebrew word *chesed*.

What do we read in Isaiah?

> For the Lord hath called thee as a woman forsaken
> and mourning in spirit, and as a wife cast off from
> her youth, said thy God. For a small moment
> have I forsaken thee, but with great mercies will I
> gather thee.
>
> In a moment of indignation have I hid my face
> a little from thee, but with everlasting kindness
> have I had mercy on thee, said the Lord thy
> Redeemer. (Isaiah 54:6–8)

Again Hosea says that the Lord does not want to be called Lord so much as "husband," since to be called Lord is to be worshipped with fear rather than love, as though He were a Baal and not a Savior. For it is characteristic of a Baal to have no *chesed*. The power of the Baal is another power, frightening and capricious, but unable to reach the depths of our own being. *Chesed* can take possession of our hearts and transform them and so it is said

> And it shall be in that day, saith the Lord, That she shall call me: My husband, and she shall call me no more Baal.
> And I will take away the names of Baalim out of her mouth, and she shall no more remember their name. (Hosea 2:16–17)

Again *chesed* is something more than mercy. But it contains in itself many varied aspects of God's love which flash forth in mercy and are its fountain and its hidden source. Remember how God revealed Himself to Moses on Sinai. First Moses had begged to see His face, and the Lord had told Moses that no one could see Him and live. Moses had pleaded to see Him, so God showed Himself without showing Himself. That is to say that Moses saw Him by not seeing Him, since he saw Him when He was gone. But He "had been" there (He who is everywhere and nowhere). That is to say that Moses having first known Him in complete darkness without seeing Him, then saw Him in a kind of light-after-darkness without knowing Him. First the dark flash and the passing and the night, then the cries and words drawn out of the depths of the darkness and mystery of that awakening. These great words shot up out of the heart of Moses and exploded in various shapes and tones which all formed the figure of *chesed*:

> O the Lord, the Lord God, merciful and gracious, patient and of much compassion and true, who keepest mercy unto thousands: who takest away

iniquity and wickedness and sin, and no man of
himself is innocent before thee. (Exodus 34:6–7)

The *chesed* of God is a gratuitous mercy that considers no
fitness, no worthiness and no return. It is the way the Lord
looks upon the guilty and with His look makes them at once
innocent. This look seems to some to be anger because they
fly from it. But if they face it they see that it is love and that
they are innocent. (Their flight and the confusion of their own
fear make them guilty in their own eyes.) The *chesed* of God
is truth. It is infallible strength. It is the love by which He
seeks and chooses His chosen, and binds them to Himself. It
is the love by which He is married to mankind, so that if humanity is faithless to Him it must still always have a fidelity
to which to return: that is His own fidelity. He has become
inseparable from man in the *chesed* which we call "Incarnation," and "Cross," and "Resurrection." He has also given us
His *chesed* in the Person of His Spirit. The Paraclete is the full,
inexpressible mystery of *chesed*. So that in the depths of our
own being there is an inexhaustible spring of mercy and of
love. Our own being has become love. Our own self has become God's love for us, and it is full of Christ, of *chesed*. But
we must face it and accept it. We must accept ourselves and
others as *chesed*. We must be to ourselves and to others signs
and sacraments of mercy.

Chesed, mercy and power, manifests itself visibly in the
chasid, or the saint. Indeed the saint is one whose whole life is
immersed in the *chesed* of God. The saint is the instrument of
the divine mercy. Through the *chasid* the love of God reaches
into the world in a visible mystery, a mystery of poverty and
love, meekness and power. The *chasid* is in many respects a
foolish one, who has been made comical by mercy. For the
apparent tragedy of his nothingness is turned inside out with
joy. In his folly the divine wisdom shines forth and his anni-
hilation is a new creation, so that he rejoices in the incongru-
ity of the divine mercies and is everlastingly astonished at
the creative love of God. He calls upon all beings to praise

this love with him, and most of them do not pay attention. Yet the sun and moon and the sea and the hills and stars join him, nevertheless, in praising *chesed*. The majority of men, perhaps, consider him crazy.

(God, too, is glad to be thought crazy in His *chasid*. For the wisdom of God is folly in the eyes of men.)

The folly of the *chasid* is manifested in his love and concern for his neighbor, the sinner. For the sinner is "next to" the *chasid* or the saint. They are so close to one another, so like one another, that they are sometimes almost indistinguishable. The professionally pious man, on the contrary, makes a whole career out of being distinguishable from sinners. He wants it to be very clear to God and to man that he and the sinner are in different categories. Hence the love of the *chasid* for the sinner (and of the sinner for the *chasid*) is not the patronizing concern of the pious and respectable, but the impractical concern of one who acts as if he thought he were the sinner's mother and brother and sister. Such a one behaves like the Samaritan in the parable, and not like the priest and Levite, who were well aware of proprieties, land classifications, and categories. Who knows? Perhaps the priest took a look at the character lying in the ditch and observed that he had blood all over him and that it would never do to contract a ritual impurity. Especially out here in the desert, miles from water. Those who are professionally respectable, and whose lives are measured out in long and formal ceremonies, have other things to do than to be instruments of *chesed*.

Who, then, is my neighbor? To whom am I bound? Whom must I love?

These are not intelligent questions, and they do not have clear answers. On the contrary any attempt to answer them involves us in endless subtleties, and vagueness, and ultimate confusion. Love knows no classifications. The measure of love that Christ has set for us is beyond measure: we must "be perfect as the heavenly Father is perfect." But what is meant by the "perfection" of the heavenly Father? It is impartiality, not in the sense of justice that measures out equally to all, knowing their merits, but in the sense of *chesed* that knows no classification of good and evil, just or unjust. "For He sends His rain upon the just and the unjust."

We are bound to God in *chesed*. The power of His mercy has taken hold of us and will not let go of us: therefore we have become foolish. We can no longer love wisely. And because we have emptied ourselves in this folly which He has sent upon us, we can be moved by His unpredictable wisdom, so that we love whom we love and we help whom we help, not according to plans of our own but according to the measure laid down for us in His hidden will, which knows no measure. In this folly, which is the work of His Spirit, we must love especially those who are helpless and who can do nothing for themselves. We must also receive love from them, realizing our own helplessness, and our own inability to fend for ourselves. *Chesed* had made us as though we were outcasts and sinners. *Chesed* has numbered us among the aliens and strangers: *chesed* has not only robbed us of our reason but declassified us along with everyone else, in the sight of God. Thus we have no home, no family, no niche in society, and no recognizable function. Nor do we even appear to be especially charitable, and we cannot pride ourselves on virtue. *Chesed* had apparently robbed us of all that, for he who lives by the mercy of God alone shall have nothing else to live by, only that mercy. *Plenitudo legis est charitas.* Mercy fulfills the whole law.

The mystery of the Good Samaritan is this, then: the mystery of *chesed*, power and mercy. In the end, it is Christ Himself who lies wounded by the roadside. It is Christ Who comes by in the person of the Samaritan. And Christ is the bond, the compassion and the understanding between them. This is how the Church is made of living stones, compacted together in mercy. Where there is on the one hand a helpless one, beaten and half dead, and on the other an outcast with no moral standing and the one leans down in pity to help the other, then there takes place a divine epiphany and awakening. There is "man," there reality is made human, and in answer to this movement of compassion a Presence is made on the earth, and the bright cloud of the majesty of God overshadows their poverty and their love. There may be no consolation in it. There may be nothing humanly charming about it. It is not necessarily like the movies. Perhaps the encounter is outwardly sordid and unattractive. But the Presence of God is brought about on earth there, and Christ is there, and God is in communion with man.

This is what we are talking about when we speak of "doing the will of God." Not only fulfilling precepts, and praying, and being holy, but being instruments of mercy, and fastening ourselves and others to God in the bonds of *chesed*.

The two questions asked by the scribe were, then, useless. Therefore Christ did not answer them. Yet He did not pass them by without attention. On the contrary, He saw them as indications of the scribe's plight and of our own. Instead of answering the question, He poured oil and wine into the wounds. This He did by His own words, Who is Himself the answer to all useful questions.

[1961]

THE NAME OF THE LORD

The author of the Epistle to the Hebrews opens his testimony concerning the High Priesthood of the Incarnate Word by contrasting God's revelation of Himself to men "through the ministry of angels" and His manifestation of Himself in His Son. The very first words of the Epistle recall the fact that "in old days God spoke to our fathers in many ways and by many means, through the prophets." But now He has spoken in a Son who inherits the universe which is also created in Him (cf. Colossians 1:16). He is the image of the Father's glory, sitting at the Father's right hand in majesty "superior to the angels as He has inherited a name Superior to theirs" (Hebrews 1:1–5). Perhaps the writer of Hebrews also had in mind the contrast that is found in the Torah between the appearances of the mysterious "malakh' Yahweh" (the angel of the Lord), and the Lord's much more pure, more immediate and more direct revelation of Himself in *His Name*, Yahweh.

As a matter of fact, in the Torah the experience of seeing, or perhaps even wrestling with the "angel of the Lord" (Genesis 32:24f) was reserved for very special individuals, and besides it had something in common with the religious experiences of the other peoples of the near East (cf. Judges 13:3–16).

The angel, however, refuses to reveal his name. He remains an anonymous manifestation of divine power in an extraordinary experience which breaks in upon the life of an individual and leaves him permanently changed (Genesis 32:25). In contrast with the vision of the Lord through His angel, is a personal confrontation with Him in and through His Name. Note however that in Exodus 23:21 the Lord tells Moses that His angel will precede Israel, *"and my Name is in him."* Here the Name of the Lord is evidently transcendent and divine, while the angel remains a created being, in and through whom the Name of the Lord is manifested by His action in saving His People.

Yet the experience of knowing and invoking the Name of Yahweh was nothing esoteric, since it was given to all the members of the holy People. Indeed, that was one of the things that made it a people, and holy. Knowing the Lord's Name, they were *His* people. His Name dwelt among them, and was invoked upon them, and was known in their midst (Exodus 23:21; Deuteronomy 12:5; I Kings 8:16–30; Numbers 6:22–27). Yet at the same time, the knowledge of the Name of the Lord definitely and clearly separated everyone who received it, from the multifarious nature cults and kingship cults of the "nations." He who "knew the Name" of Yahweh, by that fact knew the nothingness of all other gods, and was bound to "hallow" or "sanctify" the Name of Yahweh by a total obedience, fidelity and dedication that abjured any division of heart and any temptation to share the cult of Yahweh with that of another (cf. Leviticus 18:21). Any attempt to worship another god, together with Yahweh was not only a violation of the first and most important commandment, but it also "profaned the Name of Yahweh."

That God should reveal His Name to His people was the most important of all gifts, the gift which contained in itself every other gift. To bestow knowledge of His Name, was at the same time to grant His people power to enter into His presence, to invoke him, to commune with Him, to praise

Him, and to find, in the liturgical sanctification ("hallowing") of His Name, the central meaning of their own existence as His people. This was therefore something more than the revelation of knowledge "about" Himself, or even a revelation of His essence. It is a revelation of His Presence as a transcendent, personal and existential fact, indeed as the supreme actuality. And hence the Name Yahweh, even more than the other Names of God, is expressive of the divine majesty. By His Name, Yahweh would be personally present wherever He was invoked in a manner that accorded with His will, and therefore manifested fidelity to the true meaning of His Name (cf. John 14:13–14).

He would grant His People the capacity to "remember" His Name in a cult especially established by Him for this purpose. This "remembering" of the Name of Yahweh was, of course, more than a mere recalling to conscious awareness: it implied a personal confrontation in worship and the renewal of covenant obedience (Joshua 24:14–25).

The revelation of the Name Yahweh was at the same time more and less than the revelation of the Divine Essence and Attributes. More because it made God present in His personal being, in all the immediacy and urgency of a gratuitous, redemptive love. Less, because it did not give detailed knowledge of His nature.

On the other hand, the Name El-Elohim—Allah—tends to be more a revelation of the divine nature, the divine power. But this is simply the common Semitic name for God and is not a special revelation of Yahweh to His people. In fact, "El" can designate *any* God, and there are many points in common between El-Shaddai (God Almighty) in the Old Testament with the "High God" of the Canaanites (cf. Genesis 35:9–15). El-Elohim is the all-powerful creator and Lord of Nature, who manifests Himself in cosmic theophanies. Yahweh is the Lord of the "salvation-history" of the chosen People, who reveals not only His power but His unfailing mercy (*chesed*) and His fidelity (*emet*).

. To remember the Name of Yahweh was to enter into His presence in and through the all holy Name as it was invoked by the sacred assembly: but this was not merely a question of collective religious awe at the transcendent power of the divine nature, El-Shaddai, El-Elohim. It was also and above all an awareness of being in the presence of the *Person* of the Lord, Yahweh, and consequently it meant awareness of, submission to the expression of His free and personal will to glorify His Name in the midst of His people, by the saving power of His *chesed*, or unfailing love.

Even where the Lord manifested Himself, in pre-Mosaic times, through an angel, there was felt an immediate need to seek the "name" of the "man of God" who had thus appeared. Manoah, for instance, wants to offer sacrifice to the angel who has promised him the birth of a son, Samson. The angel tells him to offer sacrifice to the Lord instead. Manoah, still not comprehending the full meaning of this situation, asks: "What is your name that we may honor you when your words come true?" The angel of the Lord answered him: "Why do you ask my name, which is mysterious?" Then Manoah took the kid with a cereal offering and offered it on a rock to the Lord "whose works are mysterious" (Judges 13:18–19). (Note the following verses, to the end of the Chapter. Cf. Genesis 32; 30.)

Here in this curious text which, doubtless, reflects the confluence of a variety of primitive religious traditions, and is therefore somewhat ambiguous, we see the importance primitive men attached to the knowledge of the *Name* of any supernatural being, who might be invoked as a helper or intercessor. To call upon the Name of such a one was to enter into contact with a power greater than man's, and to know the name of that power was, in some sense, to befriend it. The life and power of an intelligent being (in the African Bantu sense of *muntu*) is mysteriously present in his name. In the case of human or angelic beings, the name exercises a power over the person himself—if he is called, he cannot help responding in some way. Yahweh can of course refuse to hear when His name is invoked, but He freely commits Himself by a promise to hear and respond when His Name is invoked by His people in the sacred assembly, or even by the faithful individual:

> Because he cleaves to me in love, I will deliver
> him;
> *I will protect him because he knows my name.*
> When he calls to me, I will answer him;
> I will be with him in trouble,
> I will rescue him and honor him.
> With long life I will satisfy him, and show him my
> salvation.
>
> (Psalms 90/91/:14–16 RSV) (cf. Psalms 9:11;
> 39/40/:5, etc.)

As for Yahweh Himself, His "name shared directly in His own holiness and was, so to speak, the double of His being."[1] Hence, to remember His Name was to enter into the presence of His awful majesty. Not only that, the Name of Yahweh was actually the "embodiment of saving revelation."[2] To remember the Name of Yahweh was to remember all His merciful and faithful promises, all His interventions in history. In a certain sense, the past, present and future came together in the invocation of the divine Name. The realization of past promises, in the saving history of the People of God merged with the hope that present needs would be met with the same unfailing fidelity and mercy as in the glorious past. In this hope they were already so to speak realized.

Thus the invocation of the Name of Yahweh in time, in the cult, and in history, implied the discovery of a dynamism in the experience of the people of God which, in later times, would take on an eschatological orientation. Thus the "sanctifications" of the Name of the Lord brought together the beginning and the end, the creation and the final judgement, and foreshadowed the establishment of the promised eschatological kingdom. In the New Testament Apocalypse, the Lord, Kurios, would declare Himself to be "the Alpha and Omega, the beginning and the end."

The primitive revelation of the Name of Yahweh at Horeb was still far from this. Nevertheless, the Name and Presence of Yahweh would remain at once the dynamic center of the life and history of God's people, and it would also theologically "take the place which in other cults was occupied by the cultic image."[3]

Yahweh was truly a "living God" because He was present, not in a dead image but in a powerful and dynamic personal presence, His Name which "dwelt in the midst of His people."

If the revelation of the Name of Yahweh had been merely the revelation of the divine nature or essence, it might in some way have become accessible to the other nations. They might have deduced it from observing nature created by Him. It might have become part of their cultic heritage and merged with their syncretistic worship built around the season cycle and the creative forces of natural life. After all, this would only have meant linking up a cosmic worship with a supreme metaphysical source, the divine nature of the Ruler of the Universe. But the revelation of the Name of Yahweh was far more than that. It was the revelation of a personal freedom intervening, with His own wise and inscrutable purposes, in the history of His own elect people. Consequently the meaning of His intervention was not accessible, and could not be accessible, to anyone who was not involved in the salvific plan of Yahweh.

The Israelite who sooner or later yielded to the temptation to identify Yahweh, more or less in good faith, with the Baalim, was in fact forgetting the purely personal character of the free, deliberate self-revelation of God in His Name. He was reverting to the concept of a divine nature: a concept which was less demanding because, precisely, it did not insist upon so serious and so earnest confrontation of hearts and wills, and hence required, instead of personal and particular obedience, only a kind of general submission to the forces implanted in nature by a divine creative, or perhaps only directive, power. The various Baals, of course, all had their proper names. But to invoke them was to invoke a *force,* and not a free and personal presence filled with the power to judge and to have mercy. A force, indeed, which might be unpredictable in its action: hence not subject to what we would call "scientific" control. Yet this unpredictability sprang not from personal freedom but from the capriciousness of a cosmic force which eludes conscious control.

The primitive revelation of the Name of Yahweh was not the revelation of a name like any other. YHWH, the "unspeakable tetragrammaton" (Origen), is in some sense not a name at all. Some scholars interpret Exodus 3:14 as a *refusal* of Yahweh to manifest His Name and identity, a rebuff to an impertinent question! This is hardly likely, when Moses is the one entrusted with the revelation of Yahweh and His plan of salvation to the chosen People. Yet there is no question that the statement "I am who I am" is in some sense evasive. In effect, Yahweh is refusing to declare or define His ineffable Nature, but is clearly and forcefully manifesting *His presence and His being as a Person* with a free and salvific plan emanating from an abyss of incomprehensible and loving mercy (cf. Exodus 34:6).

On the other hand it is certain that the form YHWH, which no one knows with certainty how to pronounce, was introduced in late Old Testament times to ensure that the Holy Name would never be treated with the slightest irreverence. Thus it ceased to be spoken at all. The Manual of Discipline of the Qumran community prescribes expulsion for a member who dared to pronounce the ineffable Name. When the Name of God was read aloud in the cult it was replaced by *Adonai* (Lord) and this was followed by the *Kyrios* of the Septuagint and the *Dominus* of the Vulgate.

Clement of Alexandria however said (*Stromateis* V.6.34), "The tetragram and mystic name which was grasped only by those to whom the impenetrable was accessible, is pronounced Ιαουε (Yahweh)."[4] A modern Biblical scholar writes: "As a primary religious feeling the name Yahweh called up the idea of the living, awe inspiring presence of God."[5] Hence we should be grateful to the editors of the *Bible de Jerusalem* for giving us the Name Yahweh everywhere instead of "Lord."

The Name Yahweh expresses the simplest, most direct and most powerful manifestation of God as *Person* in the Old Testament. The third chapter of Exodus is one of the most important texts in the Bible. It forms the basis not only for the Christian and Jewish theology, but also for the whole Religious concept of Islam. It is a text that must be known, meditated and absorbed by a believer in any one of these religions.

After the episode of the burning bush at Horeb (Exodus 3:1–12) where Moses is told that he must go and bring the Israelites out of Egypt, and that he must say he has been "sent" for this purpose, Moses understandably asks: "If they want to know who sent me, what Name shall I give them?" It is important that the "power" which offers himself for the salvation of Israel, should be identified: whether as the God of the Fathers, *or* Abraham, *or* of Isaac, *or* of Jacob (there might possibly be a choice), or as some other God. For instance He might simply be the God of this locality, Mount Horeb. The answer of Yahweh meant, among other things, that He was not the God of some particular place or tribe or natural force. In effect, it is that he is not "one of the gods." Nor is He simply a nature among natures, a being among beings. The reply in Exodus 3:14 is certainly not a statement of "what kind of being" has sent Moses into Egypt. It is a declaration of the personal and transcendent presence of the invisible one who now speaks to Moses and who will also be present with him in Egypt.

The precise meaning of this statement has considerably exercised recent scholarship. Linguistic studies have found various ways of deriving YHWH from different forms of the verb "to be." Traditionally, Catholic theology has given this a metaphysical interpretation, which is quite legitimate as a *development* of its revealed content. It is however not altogether clear that the primitive meaning of the statement corresponds exactly to the rather special implications of the Septuagint (*eimi ho on*) and the Vulgate (*Ego sum qui sum*). In these versions there is a plausible and legitimate emphasis on the declaration of the absolute aseity of God: God *is* in Himself, depending on no other being, exalted above all beings, not to be confused with any, pure being, pure act, existing purely *a se*. The Vulgate can suggest two interpretations: I am who am, in the sense of I am *He who Is*. Or, more cryptically and concretely, I am *who I am* with the implication that God thus reveals *that* He is but not *who or what He is*.

Doubtless there is in this revelation of the divine being a clear implication of aseity, infinite reality, pure actuality and eternity. God is He who is, and in contrast to His pure being, all transient things "are not." Above all, the other beings which claim to be gods are simply delusions.

Other interesting possibilities have been advanced by modern scholarship and all of them tend to be, as we would say, more "existential" than those we have just discussed.

"I am He who *causes to be*." This also could be implicitly contained in the traditional Catholic elucidation of the Septuagint and Vulgate texts.

"*I am what I will be.*" A more dynamic, less static, extrapolation of "I am what I am." "*I will be what I will be.*" This is more mysterious, and the emphasis is more dynamic still. It declares the infinite freedom of Yahweh, while at the same time focussing our attention not on His being but on His activity, since in this interpretation there seems to be an implication of what Yahweh will *be to Israel,* that is, by what acts of mercy or judgement He intends, inscrutably, to manifest Himself in Israel, and be present in the midst of Israel.

Similar to this is another interpretation which is very attractive, "I am the *one who loves passionately.*" This rests on a linguistic hypothesis which need not detain us here. Finally, Von Rad inclines to the most satisfactory interpretation in the light of present scripture studies: "I am the one Present," or perhaps "I am the one who will be present (when the crisis takes place in Egypt)."

This accords with the context, Exodus 3:12, in which the Lord says, in sending Moses to Egypt "I will be with you." But it is not redundant. Yahweh is saying that He *will be* present because He is the one who *is* present. Not that His presence is a metaphysical necessity, but a religious and transcendent fact of a quite unique character. Moses is aware of the altogether extraordinary and gratuitous reality of God's presence to him here at Horeb. This in itself constitutes and implies a promise of that same presence and powerful protection in the future. Thus the reality of Yahweh's presence is perceived not by a metaphysical intuition but by theological faith and hope and therefore it belongs not to the philosophical order, is not an awareness of *nature*, but a *personal relationship* of a supremely religious kind.

Buber brings this out in his translation: "I will be there as the *I* that will be there."

If at first sight this choice of possible interpretations seems confusing, we need not waste time trying to select one alone, to the exclusion of all the others. They are all good possibilities and hence the best thing for the average reader of the Bible to do is to take them all into account, and see them as complementary aspects of a hidden content which doubtless far exceeds them all. The very fact of these different interpretations, in their differences and in their common elements, points to an extremely clear and powerful primitive revelation of God, an experience which in its existential and spiritual impact goes beyond any other recorded in any document to which we have access, apart from the radically different revelations of God's presence and action in the New Testament. What marks this revelation out from all other records of God's manifestation of Himself to men is its special character as *personal, existential and free.*

It is in no sense a deduction from a natural experience. It is not an awareness of transcendent unity, arrived at through mystical liberation. It is even beyond what can be described, in Buber's famous term, as an "I-Thou" relationship. It is the presence of Him who is present, in a "Name" that eludes metaphysical elaboration because it is the source, the root and in some sense the embodiment of theology. However, it is not simply the root *concept* from which a theological system grows. The Name Yahweh is the source of theology in the sense that it is the living center around which the tribes of Israel gather in that unity which will enable them all to "attend to his law" (Psalm 77:1) and learn His ways while celebrating the great works of His power and of His unfailing mercy. The Name Yahweh is the heart of a living theology because, when it is invoked, the light, strength, presence, mercy and peace of Yahweh are shed upon His people. In calling upon the Name of Yahweh, they *live* their theology, or rather theology lives and works in them.

It must not however be imagined that this is reducible to a complacently nationalistic "Gott mit uns" doctrine, a sure guarantee of collective euphoria, prosperity and pride.

The presence of Yahweh can mean blessing or punishment, mercy or destruction. The living and holy Name of the Lord dwells in the midst of His people as a terrible force for judgement. Far from lending His power to the People as a means to achieve their own shortsighted political ends, Yahweh glorifies His Name by refusing to let it be a quasi-magical means subservient to man's will. Indeed, to call upon the Name of Yahweh for one's own purely secular purpose is a profanation of His Name akin to magic. In that event, the

Name of Yahweh will bring destruction upon His people, and in the cataclysm itself they "will know that I am Yahweh."

> Because the land is full of bloody crimes and the city is full of violence, I will bring the worst of the nations to take possession of their houses; I will put an end to their proud might, and their holy places shall be profaned. When anguish comes, they will seek peace, but there shall be none. Disaster comes upon disaster, rumor follows rumor; they seek a vision from the prophet, but the law perishes from the priest, and counsel from the elders. The king mourns, the prince is wrapped in despair, and the hands of the people of the land are palsied by terror. According to their way I will do to them, and according to their own judgments I will judge them; *and they shall know that I am Yahweh.* (Ezekiel 7:23–27)

> You have feared the sword; and I will bring the sword upon you, says the Lord God. And I will bring you forth out of the midst of it, and give you into the hands of foreigners, and execute judgments upon you. You shall fall by the sword; I will judge you at the border of Israel; and you shall know that I am Yahweh. This city shall not be your caldron, nor shall you be the flesh in the midst of it; I will judge you at the border of Israel; and you shall know that I am Yahweh; for you have not walked in my statutes, nor executed my ordinances, but have acted according to the ordinances of the nations that are round about you. (Ezekiel 11:8–12)

Yet at the same time the infallibly faithful mercy of Yahweh will have the last word. Even though Israel may have defiled His Name among the Gentiles (Ezekiel 36:22, 23) He will renew His people and give them new life in His Spirit, making them a new people, and thus paradoxically His "Name will be magnified among the gentiles" by His mercy to the chosen ones whom He has chastened and then brought back to Himself.

> Therefore say to the house of Israel, Thus says the Lord God: It is not for your sake, O house of Israel, that I am about to act, but for the sake of my holy name, which you have profaned among the nations to which you came. And I will vindicate the holiness of my great name, which has been profaned among the nations, and which you have profaned among them; and the nations will know that I am Yahweh, says the Lord God, when through you I vindicate my holiness before their eyes. For I will take you from the nations, and gather you from all the countries, and bring you into your own land. I will sprinkle clean water upon you, and you shall be clean from all your uncleannesses, and from all your idols I will cleanse you. A new heart I will give you, and a new spirit I will put within you; and I will take out of your flesh the heart of stone and give you a heart of flesh. And I will put my Spirit within you, and cause you to walk in my statutes and be careful to observe my ordinances. You shall dwell in the land which I gave to your fathers; and you shall be my people, and I will be your God. And I will deliver you from all your uncleannesses; and I will summon the grain and make it abundant and lay no famine upon you. I will make the fruit of the tree and the increase of the field abundant, that you may never again suffer the disgrace of famine among the nations. Then you will remember your evil ways, and your deeds that were not good; and you will loathe yourselves

for your iniquities and your abominable deeds. It
is not for your sake that I will act, says the Lord
God; let that be known to you. Be ashamed and
confounded for your ways, O house of Israel.
(Ezekiel 36:22–32)

The theme of Yahweh's Name becoming known to the
gentiles and His praise resounding to the ends of the earth is
one of the chief messages of Deutero-Isaias (Isaias 65:1; 56:1–
7, 60; cf. Michaeas 4:1–5). Here we begin to see the eschatological implications of the Name of Yahweh which will be made
known clearly to His enemies, in judgment, after a period in
which it has no longer been invoked at all (Isaias 64:2, 7) even
in Israel. Then His Name will be "great among the gentiles"
(Malachy 1:11). In the magnificent 60th chapter of Isaias, and
in the Epiphany liturgy, we see all the nations coming out
of darkness to the radiant light of Yahweh rising over Jerusalem. They are drawn to her "because of the Name of Yahweh your God and because of the holy one of Israel who has
glorified you" (Isaias 60:9). Yet this return of the light of the
divine name presupposes a period of darkness, absence and
silence, when even the People of God seems not to be His
People (Osee 1:9).

But in any case, it is for His Name's sake that Yahweh finally shows mercy (Isaias 48:9, 10), for only thus is He fully
true to the promise implied in His original revelation of Himself as the ever present and ever faithful bestower of com-
passionate and redemptive love (hesed). Hence the Name
of Yahweh once revealed, is a permanent promise of mercy
and salvation, since in revealing His Being, and giving His
Name to be invoked, Yahweh commits Himself in some sense
to save a world in which His Name is present. And because
the Name of Yahweh is present in the world even in silence,
when He is "forgotten" by the majority of men, it remains
as a dormant flame at once of judgment and of mercy, ready
to flare out at the moment determined by His inscrutable
and salvific designs. This culminating point of the salvation

history, when the Name of the Lord will resound to the ends of the earth and will be greeted by the response of universal praise, the *alleluia* of the nations, is the *Day of the Lord*, the Day of Yahweh.

At first all the earth shall be silent before Him (Sophonias 1:7), then the "word of the Lord" shall descend upon all the nations (Sophonias 2:5, etc.) to judge and purify the world, confronting false prophets who invoke His name without obeying His truth, destroying all the false gods and the power of the worldly cities (Sophonias 3). But finally, "in the day of His resurrection" the Lord will enable all the nations to call upon Him in purity of worship and in true unity, built around the "remnant" of the poor, the *anawim*, remaining as a kind of nucleus of holiness because they continued to trust in His Name when all had forgotten Him.

> "Therefore wait for me," says Yahweh,
> "for the day when I arise as a witness.
> For my decision is to gather nations,
> to assemble kingdoms,
> to pour out upon them my indignations,
> all the heat of my anger;
> for in the fire of my jealous wrath
> all the earth shall be consumed.

> "Yea, at that time I will change the speech of the
>   peoples
> to a pure speech,
> that all of them may call on the name of the
>   Yahweh
> and serve him with one accord.
> From beyond the rivers of Ethiopia
> my suppliants, the daughter of my dispersed
>   ones,
> shall bring my offerings.

"On that day you shall not be put to shame
because of the deeds by which you have rebelled
    against me;
for then I will remove from your midst
your proudly exultant ones,
and you shall no longer be haughty
in my holy mountain.
For I will leave in the midst of you
a people humble and lowly.
They shall seek refuge in the name of
Yahweh,
those who are left in Israel;
they shall do no wrong
and utter no lies,
nor shall there be found in their mouth
a deceitful tongue.
For they shall pasture and lie down,
and none shall make them afraid."

                (Sophonias 3:8–13)

You will take up this taunt against the king of
Babylon:

"How the oppressor has ceased,
the insolent fury ceased!
Yahweh has broken the staff of the wicked,
the scepter of rulers,
that smote the peoples in wrath
with unceasing blows,
that ruled the nations in anger
with unrelenting persecution . . ."

                (Isaias 14:4–6)

It is not surprising to find these same themes taken up again in the Apocalypse, where trust in the Name of the Lord is what gives the martyrs strength to remain faithful in the last great tribulations (cf. Apocalypse 2:3, 13, etc.). At the same time, however, the persecution is let loose against them precisely because of the Lord's Name, *propter nomen meum* (John 15:21). Hence the fidelity of the martyrs is summed up in the expression "to hold fast to my Name" (Apocalypse 2:13; cf. 3:11). The victory of faith is rewarded by the Name of the Lord being written upon the victorious one, who becomes a pillar in the City of God (Apocalypse 3:12, 14:1).

What is the "Name" that is thus invoked and honored in the visions of the New Testament Apocalypse? It is the Name which was given by Joseph to Mary's child, at the command of the angel (Matthew 1:21): Ye-shuah, *Yahweh saves*, or, in the form familiar to us: Jesus. Thus the Name which is said, in Hebrew, to be "inherited" by the Incarnate Word is the same "I am" revealed to Moses, present in the midst of the People of God throughout the Salvation history. That is why Jesus said, "Before Abraham was, *I am*" (John 8:58). The Christian faith then sees in the *Person* of Jesus the living, actual presence of the ineffable Name.

[1962]

"In Silentio"

A Note on Monastic Prayer

"In the beginning," says Genesis, "the earth was void and empty and darkness was upon the face of the deep; and the Spirit of God moved over the waters. And God said: *Be light made!* and light was made."

In these mysterious words which tell of the world's first beginnings, the Fathers of the Church also saw a symbolic expression of spiritual creation, and of the beginning of spiritual life in intelligent beings made to contemplate God. The spirit of man is a natural void that waits for the Spirit of God, a deep space that remains chaos until the creative Spirit of God hovers over it, and until perfect light is poured into its transparent depths by the presence of the Word, awakening man to spiritual freedom.

As soon as Adam, our first Father, came into being, these spiritual depths were filled and illuminated by the presence of God. Knowing at once that God was his Father, Adam also saw, by the same act, that the "light was good," and "divided light from darkness," order from chaos, freedom from compulsion and slavery. He knew the real from the unreal. He knew his own identity, as a spirit who had come from the creative hand of God, and lived in God, and was destined to plunge by His freedom into the infinite depths of the divine light. In this recognition, he also knew every other truth that pertained to him as a son of God. He did not therefore need to know evil, because evil did not pertain to him. The son of God need not know evil, since God, his Father, does not know evil. Nor is there any need for freedom to know what does not perfect it—and (moral, spiritual) evil is a corruption and frustration of freedom.

But when the first man spontaneously chose to experience evil and committed his freedom to an illusion, he immersed his light in darkness. His soul became a void, an abyss, a nothingness, and night descended upon the depths of his spirit. Yet in the darkness he remained famished for light, in chaos his spirit still thirsted for order and peace, and in his nonentity he could not help but to aspire to being, to spiritual liberty, to a true identity. And so man cried out for the light from which he had fled. And the Spirit of God hovered over him. But who could understand this hovering? Were these the wings of a protector or of an avenger? Was God friend or enemy? The Laws He gave to men, out of the bosom of His impenetrable hiddenness, offered no satisfactory answer.

In the fullness of time, God willed to reveal His answer to this question. He willed to show His kindness and mercy to men. He would prove that He had never ceased to love His wayward son. And to make this evident, He Himself came to seek the son who was unable to return to Him. So God sent His own Light, His Word, His only-begotten Son into the world created by Him. Thus once again He divided the light from the darkness, and recovered what was His own.

When Jesus descended into the waters of the Jordan, the Spirit of God once again moved over the waters and there was a new creation. The darkness that brooded over the face of the abyss, the image of God in man's soul, was once again dispelled. And the Spirit, hovering not only over the waters but precisely over the Son of God as He emerged from the

purified waters, made all men hear the voice of the invisible
Father speaking from heaven: "This is my beloved Son, in
whom I am well pleased" (Matthew 3:17). What happened
then? Immediately Jesus was led by the same Spirit into the
desert to be tempted by the devil.

Here, in the symbolic language of divine actions recorded in Scripture, we have the meaning of the word "vocation"
and especially of the monastic vocation. The monastic vocation is a spiritual charism, a call to a life of consecration, trial,
solitary combat, of obedience to the Holy Spirit in an eschatological battle between light and darkness. The monk too,
baptized and sealed with the Spirit of Promise, imitates the
Patriarchs, the Prophets, and Jesus Himself in a desert-life,
renouncing the world of men, their concerns and their am-
bitions, not in order to affirm and perfect himself spiritually,
but in order to serve God by submitting to trial and purification, that his inmost freedom may be perfected in truth.

The monk is a man of paradise who consecrates himself
to God by a solemn and perpetual vow in order to spend his
entire life in cultivating the spiritual Eden, the "new creation"
of space and light marvellously effected by God through the
Incarnation, Passion and Resurrection of His Son. The monk
is one who, by penance and austerity, solitude, silence, renunciation, keeps himself from forgetting that the earth of his
soul is "void and empty." By prayer and faith and contemplation, he preserves the "face of the abyss" which is his soul,
from the illusory lights of merely human wisdom, and entering with Christ into the desert, struggles with the evil that is
in the world by reason of man's sin. As Adam once received
the task of cultivating Paradise and keeping it, so now the
monk, strengthened by the invisible presence of Christ, takes
upon himself the apparently hopeless task of cultivating the
desert—the sandy wastes of the human spirit deprived of
God. The Spirit hovers over the wasteland, to bring it fertility, and the Word again pitches His tent in man's world.

The monastic vocation is therefore by its very nature a call to the wilderness, because it is a call to live in hope. The monk carries on the long tradition of waiting and hoping, the long Advent of the patriarchs and prophets: an Advent which prolongs our expectation even though the Savior has come. For though Jesus has saved the world, the fruitful waters of those four rivers of Paradise, once more made accessible by the Cross, have not yet been poured out on all mankind. Even in the souls of the baptized, there is still so much that is unfruitful, so much darkness, so much emptiness, so much barren rock. The monk leaves the world, retires to the wilderness, the forest, the mountains, the lonely shores of the sea: and there, descending by his prayer into the empty spaces of his own spirit, he waits for the fulfillment of the divine promises: "The land that was desolate and impassable shall be glad, and the wilderness shall rejoice and shall flourish like the lily" (Isaias 35:1).

The monk is a man of sorrow, a man discontented with every illusion, aware of his own poverty, impatient of evasion, who seeks the naked realities that only the desert can reveal. But the monk is also a man of joy, a man at peace with the emptiness of the wilderness, glad of his limitations, loving reality as he finds it, and therefore secure in his humility. He is a man of joy and a man of sorrow both together because he is a man of desires. And because he lives by pure hope, he has entered into the secret which Christ has taught His chosen ones: that hope gives us, even on earth, the secure possession of our inestimable heritage as sons of God. What is this inheritance, and what is this possession? It is the wisdom by which we find God in the Mystery of His Christ. It is the wisdom given by His Spirit to those who have left all things to follow Him—the wisdom of the Cross. By this wisdom, the eyes of our mind are enlightened not with speculative science but with the obscure existential knowledge begotten of love, whose eyes penetrate the inner meaning of the hope that is offered to us in the Cross of Christ. This gift of loving wisdom whose very poverty endows it with vision to penetrate the mystery of God, is what St. Paul calls "the spirit of wisdom and revelation in deep knowledge of Him . . . so that you may know what is the hope of His calling, what the riches of the glory of his inheritance in the saints, and what the exceeding greatness of his power toward us who believe" (Ephesians 1:17–19).

This wisdom is no esoteric secret that can be discovered by strange and arduous techniques. It cannot be won by ascetic macerations. It cannot be learned by man's intelligence alone. It is hidden in God, for no one knows Who God really is except God, and those to whom He reveals Himself.

This wisdom which (as the prophet says) the "giants could not discover," and which the angelic spirits cannot claim as their own acquisition, is more hidden than the veins of iron and gold which have their secret beginnings in the deep recesses of the earth. The source of wisdom, from which all men desire to drink (for all men desire happiness, and wisdom is man's happiness), cannot be discovered by the rod of the diviner. Who shall tell a man the way to this hidden fountain, springing up from beyond the inmost essence of things?

"The depth said: it is not in me and the sea saith, it is not with me . . . It is hid from the eyes of all the living and the fowls of the air know it not. Death and destruction have said: with our ears we have heard the fame thereof" (Job 28:14; 21:22).

And yet, paradoxically, this wisdom cries out in the streets, and waits for men, calling to them and beckoning in the gates of the city and in the market place. But men pass by without finding wisdom. For in order to find her they must hide her commandments in their heart (Proverbs 2:1) by "keeping" them. For that is what it means, to "keep" a commandment. It means not only to remember it, but to make it part of one's own being by doing what it says.

The wisdom of God, which is spoken by the apostles "in a mystery," is a wisdom which is hidden, but revealed by the

Spirit of God. And the Spirit Himself is hidden. Nor is His voice heard with the ears.

No escape from paradox: Wisdom manifests itself, and is yet hidden. The more it hides, the more it is manifest, and the more it is manifest the more it is hidden. For God is known when He is apprehended as unknown, and He is heard when we realize that we do not know the sound of His voice. The words He utters are words full of silence, and they are bait to draw us into silence. The truths He manifests are full of hiddenness, and their function is to hide us, with themselves, in God from whom they proceed. If we hide the precepts of His wisdom in our heart—precepts of humility, meekness, charity, renunciation, faith, prayer—they themselves will hide us in Him. For the values which these virtues communicate to us, the life which they give to us, are completely hidden from the eyes of men. They bring us to the source of a life that is unknown to the natural wisdom of man, and yet from this source Man's nature itself proceeds, is nourished and is sustained. Thus the hidden things that are communicated to us in the words and precepts of the Gospel transform our lives and raise them from the level of distinct knowledge and clear evidence, natural prudence and plain practicality, to another level which is hidden and obscure to the mind of man.

What is the effect of this hiddenness? To some it seems like ignorance and despair. But to those whose vocation it is, this silence of God is a *docta ignorantia,* a learned ignorance, and a "despair" that is the mask of perfect hope. Hope, too, is hidden in silence.

To be ravished from the world of men by the silence of God means, in the end, not that one finds a new and mysterious universe to live in, but that the old, ordinary universe, with all its everyday poverty and charm, while remaining perfectly ordinary, perfectly real, perfectly poor, becomes transfigured from within by a silence which is the supreme and infinite "poverty" of an infinitely rich and generous God!

Formed by the discipline of a hidden wisdom, monks become themselves as hidden as wisdom is herself. They remain in this mortal life, and yet their life is already hidden with Christ in God and their citizenship is in heaven. They do not expect to be understood by men because they do not fully understand themselves. They realize that their silence is something of a problem and a scandal to those who happen to notice it: but they cannot fully explain the mystery to anyone. They are, themselves, too much a part of the mystery of silence to be able to formulate an apologetic for their own lives. Like wisdom, they manifest themselves by remaining hidden.

That is why it is very important to remember that the monk, the solitary, cannot clearly explain himself to the rest of the world, and he is very foolish if he attempts to do so. What a tragedy for a monk to expound what he conceives to be a clear, definite, easily understandable explanation for his monastic life, for his vocation to be hidden in God! That means he has made the mistake of convincing himself that he understands the mystery of his vocation. Does he really understand? Then there is no more mystery! And if there is no more mystery, are we not perhaps forced to say there is no longer any vocation?

What is the monastic vocation? The monk is called to enter into the hiddenness and the silence of God. Does he think he knows what that means? Perhaps in the beginning, if he does not exactly think he already knows all about his vocation, he assumes he soon will. But understanding the monastic vocation is not a mere matter of absorbing what has been written about it in books, even by the saints. Words are only the threshold of the mystery, and the silence of God's love, selecting a soul for this strange life hidden in Himself, is too vast an ocean to be lapped up by the human tongue.

And so, even though every monk remembers from his novitiate the concepts and the explanations that seem to "contain" the meaning of his vocation, as life goes on, and as he enters more deeply into his vocation, he realizes that he is far out of his depth, and that he can no longer be firmly supported by any concept or formula, however traditional, however sacred. If he cannot even explain it to himself, how can he explain it to others?

The monastic life cannot be defined by any one of its parts. It cannot be reduced to one of its aspects, any more than the life of any living organism can be fully explained by one of the vital functions which that organism performs. Man is a rational animal, they say. But he does not exist merely in order to grow, or eat, or work, or think, or even to love. On the contrary, growth, nutrition, work, thought and love all unite in promoting and increasing the existential depth of that mysterious reality which is the individual person, a concrete, free, inexplicable being endowed with powers whose depth no mind but God's can ever fathom. The human person, then, is a free being created with capacities that can only be fulfilled by the vision of an unknown God. And the monk is a person who has been unable to resist the need to seek this unknown God in the hiddenness and silence of His own inscrutable wisdom.

All the substance of the monastic vocation, therefore, is buried in the silence where God and the soul meet, not as object and subject, but as "one Spirit." The very essence of monasticism is hidden in the existential darkness of life itself. And life is inexplicable, irreducible to systematic terms. It is only understood by being lived. The best we can say is that the monk is one who goes out to the frontiers of liberty and of existence, seeking the impossible, seeking the vision which no man can see without dying. And yet this idea must immediately be corrected, for it is at once exaggerated and misleading. For when the monk is able to reach a certain degree of wisdom, he realizes that he had already found God by becoming mysteriously unwise. And then the circle is closed, and the monastic life begins.

The terrible human aspiration that reaches out over the abyss is calmed. The terror of God is so far beyond all conceivable terror that it ceases to terrify and then suddenly becomes friendly. Then, at last, begins the utterly unbelievable consolation, the consolation into which we enter through the door of an apparent despair: the deep conviction, as impossible to explain as it is to resist, that in the depths of our uselessness and futility we are one with God. "He who is joined to the Lord is one spirit." We have found Him in the abyss of our own poverty—not in a horrible night, not in a tragic immolation, but simply in the ordinary uninteresting actuality of our own everyday life.

Then, in the deep silence, wisdom begins to sing her unending, sunlit, inexpressible song: the private song she sings to the solitary soul. It is his own song and hers—the unique, irreplaceable song that each soul sings for himself with the unknown Spirit, as he sits on the doorstep of his own being, the place where his existence opens out into the abyss of God's nameless, limitless freedom. It is the song that each one of us must sing, the song of grace that God has composed Himself, that He may sing it within us. It is the song of His mercy for *us*, which, if we do not listen to it, will never be sung. And if we do not join with God in singing this song, we will never be fully real: for it is the song of our own life welling up like a stream out of the very heart of God's creative and redemptive love.

Now each man's individual song, that he sings in secret with the Spirit of God, blends also in secret with the unheard notes of every other individual song. The voices of all the men who love God, the living and the dead, those who are on earth, those who suffer in the place of probation, those who have gone into the place of victory and rest: these voices all form a great choir whose music is heard only in the depths of silence, because it is more silent than the silence itself.

[1955]

COMMUNITY OF PARDON

God reveals Himself to the world in the Mystical Christ, the Church, which is the community of those who are reconciled to the Father, in Christ, because they are united with one another in the Holy Spirit. If the unity of Christians in One Body makes the Church a sign of God in the world, and if men tend unfortunately to conflict and division by reason of their weakness, selfishness and sin, then the will to reconciliation and pardon is necessary if the Church is to make God visible in the world. Nor can this pardon, this communion in forgiveness, remain interior and invisible. It must be clearly manifest. So the mystery of the Church demands that Christians love one another in a visible and concrete way—and that they love all men.

Christ will not be visible to the world in His Church except in proportion as Christians seek peace and unity with one another and with all men. But since conflict is inevitable, unity cannot be maintained except in great difficulty, with constantly renewed sacrifice, with lucid honesty, openness, humility, the readiness to ask forgiveness and to forgive. Christian life is a perpetual conversion, a turning to God and to the Church of pardon.

In so far as the Church is a community of pardon it is an epiphany of the Divine Love, Agape: the Love that underlies the mystery of creation and of redemption. This love is the key to everything, but it cannot be known, discovered or understood by rational investigation alone. It must be revealed to men in a free gift of God. It is revealed to them in the gift of love. God has willed that men should know Him not in esoteric secrets and strange philosophies, but in the announcement of the Gospel message which is the message of His love. "This is my commandment, that you love one another as I have loved you" (John 15:12). "You have not chosen me but I have chosen you, and have appointed you that you should go and bear fruit . . . These things I command you that you may love one another" (id. 16–17). The love of Christians, commanded by God and carried out by them, makes them "God's workmanship" (Ephesians 2:10).

This is more than a message, for if it remains only a matter of words it cannot be fully received and fully understood. The word of the Gospel is understood only when it is obeyed. It is known to those who strive to practice it. Yet it is also more than a moral doctrine that can be preached by example. To receive the word of the Gospel, the Kerygma of God's love for man in Christ, of God's gift of Himself to man in Christ, is to enter into the living and active communion of love which has become the center of salvation history. This communion itself is a profound religious mystery, for it is participation not only in a natural love of man for his brother, but in the love of God for sinful man as revealed in the mystery of the Cross and Resurrection of Jesus Christ.

To enter fully into this mystery one must receive the Holy Spirit, who is the Love of God (I Corinthians 2:10–12). The Holy Spirit dwells in the Church, giving life to all who live in Christ, as members of His Church. The Holy Spirit gives light and love to those who are enlightened by the word of the Gospel and who seek truth and life in Jesus Christ. The Holy Spirit, Who is the bond of union between the Father and the

Son, is also the bond of union between the faithful who have been reconciled to the Father through the Son, and with one another in the Church.

Before His death on the Cross, Jesus told His disciples that He would soon come to them not visibly but in the Holy Spirit, and would dwell in them by His Spirit. "I will not leave you orphans, I will come to you. Yet a little while and the world no longer sees me. But you see me, for I live and you shall live. In that day you shall know that I am in the Father, and you in me and I in you" (John 14:18–20). "When the Advocate (the Paraclete, the Holy Spirit) has come, whom I will send you from the Father, the Spirit of Truth who proceeds from the Father, he will bear witness concerning me" (John 15:26–27).

As Christ passed through death to life in the Spirit (I Peter 3:18) so the Christian follows Christ on His Paschal Mystery through death to life. Sin is pardoned, man is redeemed not by the destruction and punishment of man's freedom, but by its purification.

It is precisely in his *freedom* that man accepts the redemptive power of the Cross. It is man's freedom that is nailed to the Cross with Christ and rises to new life in the Christian agape. That is to say that each individual renounces what is purely selfish and confesses his wrong, in order to find himself on the new spiritual level of reconciliation in Christ. But no one sincerely confesses his own sin without at the same time pardoning his brother (Matthew 18:23–35). Forgiveness of sins is proclaimed to the world in Christ, and is granted to each one who, in the act of seeking pardon, himself pardons others and makes himself an instrument of the divine mercy. Sin cannot be pardoned and healed without love, because all sin is, at its root, a refusal of love. No matter how great our sin may be, it is forgiven when we consent to love (Luke 7:47). The Sacrament of penance is instituted as the visible sign of this reconciliation and hence it is required that we receive it before we return from mortal sin to Eucharistic Communion, the sign of our life in Christ's love.

The Gospel is then a message of reconciliation in the Spirit of Love. Those who receive the Holy Spirit are reconciled to God and to one another in love. The supreme purpose of all life is then to receive the Holy Spirit, to live by the Spirit of Christ, to have Him dwelling and acting in our hearts (John 7:37–39). And it is for this that the Spirit awakens in our hearts faith in Christ and draws us to the Church, which is the Living Body of Christ. When we live as members of Christ, we receive the Holy Spirit. The sacraments of the Church give us participation in the life of the Spirit. Faith awakens that life in our hearts. Love is the guarantee that the life of the Spirit is growing in us. He who confesses Christ and loves his brother, who forgets himself in order to help his brother and who devotes his life to the truth of the Gospel, lives and grows in the Spirit. Love is the sign of the Holy Spirit at work in the Church and in the world.

"Everyone who loves is born of God, and knows God. He who does not love, does not know God; for God is love. In this has the love of God been shown in our case, that God has sent His only begotten Son into the world that we may live through Him. In this is the love, not that we have loved God, but that He has first loved us, and sent His Son a propitiation for our sins. Beloved, if God has so loved us, we also ought to love one another. No one has ever seen God. If we love one another, God abides in us and His love is perfected in us. In this we know that we abide in Him and He in us, *because He has given us of His Spirit*" (I John 4:7–13).

But we are not yet perfect in love. As long as we are on earth we remain sinful and imperfect men. Even though the Holy Spirit dwells in the hearts of all who have faith in Christ and seek to keep His commandment of love, yet at the same time there is in these hearts the capacity and indeed the tendency to sin. Not only that, but those who love God sincerely can still, through weakness, error, confusion, and infidelity, fall into sin. This is in fact the great problem and scandal of Christian frailty. Yet it should not be a scandal. It becomes a scandal when the true nature of the Church as a community of pardon and reconciliation is obscured, and when it is replaced by the idea of a Church that saves sinners without herself being composed of men capable of sin, indeed of sinners.

There are certainly the Gospel parables which show us the Church made up of wheat and cockle, wise and foolish virgins. But this is not the same as saying that the Church is divided into two easily recognizable *classes* of saints and sinners—as if one were more or less predestined to live a life clearly defined as being one or the other. Certainly there are men and women in the Church, both religious and laypeople, who live holy lives and avoid all serious sin. It is obligatory for all Christians to seek to live without sin. And yet the fact remains that however virtuous we may be, our virtues do not deliver us from the condition of "sinners" who often fail, make mistakes, give in to frailty, or allow ourselves to be deceived by appearances of good. No man is infallible and impeccable. We all need the mercy of God, we all need the pardon and love of our neighbor.

Furthermore all *realize,* or should realize, this frailty and fallibility in themselves. All should *feel* in the depths of their heart the accusing presence of nothingness and death which gives the lie to their vain image of themselves, their foolish and unsubstantial projects for a happiness centered in themselves. In fact, the lives of those who have been truly close to God have taught us that the saints are the ones who more than all others felt in themselves the evil of sin and the need for pardon.

The Church militant then is entirely made up of men who recognize themselves to be sinners in need of reconciliation and pardon, and not of two impossible classes: those who have become impeccable and can judge others, and those who are trying (or should try) to become impeccable so that they will not be judged any more by the perfect.

But where shall the sinner turn for pardon? To God, obviously. And the first thing is of course to seek Him in the depths of our heart, asking pardon for our sins. But the Christian conscience, enlightened by the Holy Spirit, tells us that this inner movement of repentance in the privacy of the heart, though it is essential, is not enough by itself. For sin is not a purely individual affair, and neither is pardon. However private it may be, sin remains in some sense everybody's business because everyone is affected by the evil that is in the heart of one. It is not possible for man to live so separated from others, so isolated and private in his own heart, that his secret selfishness and sin will not affect others. We are involved in each other's lives, not by choice but by necessity, for that is the way we are made. No man can pretend successfully to live purely in his own private universe and remain sane. The very condition of normal human life is community, communication, and "conversation" in the old Latin sense of *conversatio,* exchange on the level of social living. The lives of all men are inextricably mixed together, and the salvation and damnation of souls is involved in this inescapable communication of freedoms. Either we will love and help one another or we will hate and attack one another, in which latter case we will all be one another's hell. Perhaps Sartre was not far wrong in saying that where freedom is abused, society itself turns into hell. ("*L'enfer c'est les autres.*")

The heart of the Christian message is precisely reconciliation in the Spirit of Love so that communion in freedom turns to communion in beatitude. In which case heaven is communion with "others."

Therefore the Church possesses a great gift of God in the Sacrament of Penance. The sinner confesses his sin to another man who, however, listens to his confession not as man but as a representative of Christ, indeed as Christ. Because our sins concern the whole Body of Christ they must be confessed to another and forgiven by another in order for our reconciliation to Christ in His Church to be complete. And in this Sacrament the Holy Spirit is given to the forgiven one. He is restored to life in Christ. His spirit is healed by the presence of the Divine Paraclete. He can return to the altar of God and renew his spiritual joy in the Eucharistic banquet.

2.

We must in all things seek God. But we do not seek Him the way we seek a lost object, a "thing." He is present to us in our heart, our personal subjectivity, and to seek Him is to recognize this fact. Yet we cannot be aware of it as a reality unless He reveals His presence to us. He does not reveal Himself simply in our own heart. He reveals Himself to us through one another. He reveals Himself to us in the Church, in the community of believers, in the *koinonia* of those who trust Him and love Him. Seeking God is not just an operation of the intellect, or even a contemplative illumination of the mind. We seek God by striving to surrender ourselves to Him whom we do not see, but Who is in all things and through all things and above all things.

We seek God by surrendering ourselves to His will. But His will is not just a matter of blind decrees and laws external to ourselves. It is the law of love which is implanted in every nature, and the revelation of spiritual love in personal freedom. The fruit of this love is the restoration of all things in Christ, the union of all beings with God, through man, by the exercise of man's freedom.

Man's freedom is therefore the instrument of divine redemption and reconciliation. This work of reconciliation requires the formation of a living body of men who are united by the Spirit of God. God's work is to form a living mystical body, which will be His Son, the One Christ, Head and Members, in which all the members share One Spirit, one Sonship, and are "One Christ."

For this, each member must undergo a transformation by the Holy Spirit. He must undergo a renewal in the depths of his being:

> Now this I affirm and testify in the Lord, that you must no longer live as the Gentiles do, in the futility of their minds; they are darkened in their understanding, alienated from the life of God because of the ignorance that is in them, due to their hardness of heart; they have become callous and have given themselves up to licentiousness, greedy to practice every kind of uncleanness. You did not so learn Christ!—assuming that you have heard about him and were taught in him, as the truth is in Jesus. Put off your old nature which belongs to your former manner of life and is corrupt through deceitful lusts, and be renewed in the spirit of your minds, and put on the new nature, created after the likeness of God in true righteousness and holiness. (Ephesians 4:17–25)

This renewal is to be seen from many points of view: as renunciation, as pardon, as conversion, as "justification," as self-surrender, as thanksgiving, "eucharistia." The word "love" in the sense of Agape perfectly covers and includes them all.

But let us remember especially that the Church is a community of pardon. All who have entered the common life of the body of Christ have done so by the way of pardon. And they remain in the Body of Christ only through pardon, through the mercy of Christ: not only of Christ, as Head, but also of Christ in His members.

The mercy and pardon of Christ must be continually at work in all the members and through all the members of the Mystical Body. This is what makes the Church truly a Mother: she gives life by gentleness, understanding, love and pardon. She forgives sins, that is to say she heals separations. Sin is separation from God, and from those who love God. Sin is a cutting off from life. It is a spiritual death, and pardon is the restoration of life. Sin is a cutting off of man's free will from communion in love and common understanding. Sin is the refusal to share, and the denial of any need to share. Pardon renews sharing, because it brings the sinner back into contact with the body which he needs, with those whose love he needs, by whose love he lives. But the sinner is also important to the Church, for the community of pardon needs the sinner and that is why she pardons him. The Church needs to share with him the good that she has received from God.

This is why the Risen Savior, on the day of His resurrection, in His first meeting with the disciples, before all else gave them the Holy Spirit and the power to grant divine pardon:

> On the evening of that day, the first day of the week, the doors being shut where the disciples were, for fear of the Jews, Jesus came and stood among them and said to them, "Peace be with you." When he had said this, he showed them his hands and his side. Then the disciples were glad when they saw the Lord. Jesus said to them again, "Peace be with you. As the Father has sent me, even so I send you." And when he had said this, he breathed on them, and said to them, "Receive the Holy Spirit. If you forgive the sins of any, they are forgiven; if you retain the sins of any, they are retained." (John 20:19–23)

This is to be seen not only as the institution of the Sacrament of Penance, which of course it is, but also as a revelation of the truth that the very life of the Body of Christ is pardon. The Spirit by which the Church lives is the Spirit of love, of unity. Unity can be preserved or restored only by understanding, acceptance and pardon. The Church is a body of men who know they are forgiven and who forgive repeatedly because they are themselves forgiven repeatedly.

The Church is then not so much a body of men who are pure and never offend, but of men who, in their weakness and frailty, frequently err and offend, but who have received from God the power to forgive one another in His name. They possess the Holy Spirit and they can give the Holy Spirit in some sense, to one another. The Holy Spirit Himself moves them to do this, and acts in them, to save others (see Acts 8:14–18, 26–39; 10:24–48, etc.).

We, then, who form one body in Christ, share with one another the message of Christ's divine truth, we share His word, we share His worship, we share His love, we share His Spirit.

The highest adoration we offer to God, "in spirit and in truth" is in this sharing of the breath of the Divine Spirit with one another in pardon and in love. That is why we are told to forgive our brother before we go to offer sacrifice. That is why we exchange the kiss of peace before Communion. The kiss of peace is in some way a part of our Eucharistic communion: it symbolizes the spiritual sharing of the Holy Spirit. With a holy kiss we give the Holy Spirit to our brother, as if the flame of one candle were transferred to enlighten another.

The Eucharist is the celebration of our reconciliation in Christ and in His Spirit. In the Postcommunion of the Easter Mass, the Church prays God to "Pour forth upon us the Spirit of Your love, so that You may, in Your mercy, lead those who have received the Paschal Sacraments to be of one heart." Furthermore, the Holy Spirit not only renews the hearts of all the faithful through the Eucharistic liturgy and communion, but in that Liturgy the Holy Spirit Himself is given as the remission of our sins—*quia ipse est remissio omnium peccatorum* (Postcommunion, Tuesday of Pentecost). In proportion as we love and pardon one another we open the whole Church to the action of the Spirit of God.

We are a community of pardon, therefore a community of penitents. But what is a penitent? Is he simply one who carries out all kinds of difficult and forbidding acts of self-punishment? This perhaps may have a place in some lives. But the true spirit of penance is inseparable from the recognition of our need for pardon, not only of God's pardon, but of our brother's pardon. We must recognize our need for the "kiss of peace" by which our brother, in his forgiveness, and his acceptance, gives us the Holy Spirit from his own heart and in which we, in our turn, share with him the love of the Holy Spirit in our own heart.

We are a community of pardon, not a community of judgment. We are told not to judge one another, and we must not. We must not judge in such a way as to reject and condemn. That is to say we must not refuse to accept the genuine good will of our brother, we must not reject his sincere and open offers of reconciliation, his true friendship. Even our enemy must not be judged, but his need for forgiveness must be recognized. We must not judge, that is to say we must always be ready to take the first step in offering reconciliation and pardon. We must not let our evaluation of a man's acts stand in the way of the Holy Spirit, who draws us to unity with the "other" in spite of his actions which make him different from ourselves, perhaps opposed to us.

We have a duty to pardon, because it is through us that God wishes to pardon all sinners.

In building a community of pardon which is the temple of God, we have to recognize that no one of us is complete, self-sufficient, perfectly holy in himself. No one can rest in his own individual virtues and interior life. No man lives for himself alone. To live for oneself alone is to die. We grow and flourish in our own lives in so far as we live for others and through others. What we ourselves lack, God has given them. They must complete us where we are deficient. Hence we must always remain open to one another so that we can always share with each other.

Often the good that is given us by God is given us only to be shared with another. If He sees that we will not pardon and will not be open, that we will not share, then the good is not given us. But to him in whom there is the greatest readiness to share with all, most is given. The greatest of gifts then is this openness, this love, this readiness to accept and to pardon and to share with others, in the Spirit of Christ. If we are open we will not only offer pardon, but will not disdain to seek it and recognize our own desperate need of it.

Openness is the sign of the Spirit's presence, for openness is the sign of love. How characteristic was the action of Pope John XXIII who, when asked after his election what he intended to do as Pope, simply walked over to a window and flung it open.

[1963]

LITURGICAL RENEWAL: THE OPEN APPROACH

What is meant by liturgical renewal, and what are some of the problems involved? We, the ordinary clergy and laity, the commoners in the "people of God" need to understand this well, because the main job of renewal is ours. Liturgical reform merely from the top down, renewal by juridical *fiat* alone, is not really likely to work. Yet this is apparently the way many are expecting it to "happen."

Those who are passionately dedicated to the liturgical movement may perhaps be attaching too much importance to the fact that certain desirable changes have been, will be, or at any rate always *can* be legislated. But, as we are aware from the civil rights conflict, the mere opening of new ways by law does not mean that one can always travel them in fact. Hence those who are not so enthusiastic about liturgical renewal are perhaps consoling themselves with stoical reflections on the unwillingness and incapacity of most priests and laypeople to make the required changes in such a way as to effect a real and basic renewal of worship.

Changes are certainly being made. There can be no question that now, after nearly a year of the "new Mass," the changes are pointing in the right direction. Obviously the reform has only begun. The "new Mass," as it now stands, seems to represent certain practical compromises that were needed in order that a certain amount of vernacular might be allowed. But it certainly does seem illogical to switch from English to Latin just for the Prayer and then go back to English for the Epistle; or to say "The Lord be with you" now in English and now in Latin. The logic of Liturgical renewal certainly requires that the entire Mass be said in the language of the people, and this must eventually come. At the same time we may remark in passing that the old Roman, Ambrosian and other liturgies in Latin can and should be preserved in some monasteries that might be willing to dedicate themselves to this work (Solesmes, for example).

The best thing about the "new Mass" is the real opening up of opportunities for participation. With the altar now facing the people, there is obviously more sense of communication on both sides, and much less danger of the old woolgathering distractedness which always threatens the man who is merely absorbed in his own routine thoughts and imaginings. Communication being consciously established and maintained, priest and people can more easily become aware that they are together *celebrating* the mystery of our Redemption in the Eucharistic Sacrifice and the Lord's Supper.

The presence of a lay-commentator telling people when to stand, sit, and so on, and offering capsule explanations of what is going on, is of course a temporary expedient. It is not to be regarded as an unmixed blessing and the sooner everyone is able to get along without it, the better. But of course it is most desirable that a layman should participate by reading the Epistle, for example.

Concelebration and Communion under both species have been among the most impressive and praiseworthy additions to the new Liturgy, but concelebration is still of necessity confined mostly to monastic communities.

Obviously all is not yet perfect. Those who imagined that it was enough to have the texts translated into the vernacular were perhaps unprepared for the problems that might still remain. Our Bible readings are now in English. But what English! A text is being used that was prepared for private reading and study, and its attempts at bright colloquialism do not stand up well under the exigencies of public and solemn celebration. A certain sacred and timeless seriousness is required in our vernacular liturgical texts, or they will rapidly become unbearably trite.

Complaints are made about the hymn singing, and doubtless it is not always up to the standard of Gregorian. But at least it is something that everyone can do. How many parishes were there, before the Council, where *all* the congregation knew how to sing the common of the Mass in Gregorian?

There remains very much to be done. We are in a period of transition. Neither misplaced enthusiasms nor resentful non-participation will help the Church now. We must go forward in a spirit of sober and reasonable experimentation, and this means facing the hazards of trial and error. No matter what changes are made, if they are only new gestures performed in the old spirit, they will not constitute a liturgical renewal. It is not the old forms that must go so much as the old spirit. So let us take a quick look at the "old spirit," fully aware that it does not belong only to the past. It is still very much with us, even with some of those who favor progressive ideas!

Brevity always involves some risk of caricature, but obviously not much paper needs to be wasted on the familiar rigidities, the inarticulate, cramped, official and antiquated style of common worship before Vatican II. The defects are not so much in the style itself as in the psychological residue which years of this kind of worship have accumulated in the spirituality and the performance of priest and people. Incapacity to communicate together and indeed a general lack of desire to communicate all add up to a kind of consecrated bashfulness. Sacraments which imply a full, deep, open-hearted sharing in personal warmth and love, have actually become signs of a consecrated impersonality and of business-like despatch.

What difference does it make if the priest says the whole canon out loud if it still means something like this: "I am the priest, you are the laity, and this is a strictly business deal. You have your place and I have mine. I am here to confect valid sacraments for you to receive and you are there because if you were not there I would not be here confecting sacraments. Besides everyone knows that unless I exercise my special office as the only one who can validly make Our Lord sacramentally present, you won't even have a religion. Indeed you will be, for all intents, and purposes, godless. As to who you are or what you think about all this, I couldn't care less. So let's get the whole thing over with so that I can go mind my business and you yours."

This is the mentality which one of our best liturgists, Dom Adrien Nocent, has called "validism." According to this outlook, what matters is not that the ceremonies have meaning, or that the sacraments eloquently speak the grace which they signify, or that the order and comeliness of worship should help to manifest the splendor of God's love and of His presence in the midst of His people. All that matters is that the sacraments be valid, the formulas correct, and the gestures rubrically exact. Worship is mechanically efficient, the worshipper gets grace with a minimum of trouble, and all goes smoothly!

This mentality is responsible for a deadly atmosphere of officialism in cult, a pervasive and deadening influence which one is expected to counteract by interior and subjective worship, governed entirely by one's own individual tastes and needs and which, in the last analysis, is one's own responsibility and nobody else's business.

Let me say at once that this private realm of sincerity and personal awareness is not to be scoffed at. Where worship is cold, formal, official and empty of personal communication, what other refuge is left for the worshipper? I am not too sure I think it is a good thing to make him feel guilty about it, unless you have something better to offer here and now, in the concrete and not just on paper or in your own head.

What is required above all is a new spirit of *openness*, in which the priest is open to his people, and they are open to him and one another. This means that the words of the liturgy should be spoken by a person, to persons, and not just uttered abstractly in a sacred void.

It is true, and this is sometimes forgotten, that the words of the Liturgy are sacred and the people are gathered in a "sacred space." "The Lord be with you" is something else again than "Hello gang!" So the whole idea of "renewal" means something else than saying the formulas of prayer in a familiar language and with the intonations of colloquial and rotarian togetherness. It means discovering a *new* sense of sacred space, of community, of oneness in the Spirit, as a result of a communication on a deep level with which we have long ceased to be familiar: it means learning to experience the mystery of oneness in grace. This demands a community presence and awareness that is distinct from our ordinary assemblies: a presence to one another in Christ. A presence also in celebration. It means therefore a sense of mystery. One cannot possibly experience this liturgical presence and oneness if one is not open to the reality of the Spirit in and through all who have been brought together in the worshipping assembly. Yet this sense is not mystical and esoteric. It is based on our natural human affinities for one another as beings with the same needs, the same joys, the same hopes, fears and loves, who have been brought together by the merciful love of Christ. The words, songs, ceremonies, signs, movements of worship are all designed, by their very nature, to open the mind and heart of the participant to this experience of oneness in Christ. But this sacramental consciousness depends first of all on human sympathy, relatedness and on some degree of mutual understanding. Hence the obligation to be at peace with all before going to worship.

One reason why I am a Catholic, a monk and a priest today is that I first went to Mass, and kept going to Mass, in a Church where these things were realized. No matter how progressive Father Ford may have been (and, thank God, still is), Corpus Christi Church had the same Roman liturgy as everyone else in 1938. It was just the familiar Mass that is now being radically reformed. There was nothing new or revolutionary about it; only that everything was well done, not out of aestheticism or rubrical obsessiveness, but out of love for God and His truth. It would certainly be ingratitude of me if I did not remember the atmosphere of joy, light, and at least relative openness and spontaneity that filled Corpus Christi at solemn High Mass.

One of the extraordinary things about Corpus Christi Church is that it unashamedly goes back to a rather dim period in worship and art. The sanctuary has a seventeenth-century look. But it is the air of Caroline Anglicanism as well as of Baroque Catholicity. It has no baroque excess about it, but it is consciously splendid, in an honest, forthright way. I suppose the particular truthfulness of Corpus Christi is that it is one of the few Catholic Churches in America that has had the courage to look "Colonial" and "Early American" without fear of being labelled "Protestant." There is enough about the tabernacle, candlesticks, and the ritual itself that is purely Roman, Post-Tridentine Roman. The paradox is then that here was a progressive who was able to get more out of all the things the conservatives claim to prize than the conservatives themselves!

So it is not the style that matters but the spirit, the taste, the living sense of rightness and of truth, and basically the respect for God's creation, God's people, God's house. Where these are found, there is also inevitably a natural and supernatural openness, because we are made in such a way that we respond to such order and such harmony by opening our hearts and lifting them up to the light.

I remember also the side altar in the Lady Chapel at Corpus Christi with its lovely primitive Italian tryptich, its painted wooden Mexican candlesticks, its rich antependium, all these things which will probably "have to go." It does not matter. Whatever may be the rite or the style, there is none that cannot be redeemed by a certain openness, innocence, awareness, light and trust. But to say this is not to exempt from reform those styles which tend by their nature to favor rigidity and therefore to close the heart and mind to a genuine and more open participation in the liturgical mystery.

But let us be quite clear what we are participating *in*. Is Christian worship to be communion in correctness or communion in love? Oneness in Law or oneness in Christ? Sharing in valid sacraments or in the Spirit of Life that is in the Risen Savior? Certainly we must be correct, we must intelligently obey the laws of the Church and we must be concerned with the validity of the sacraments: but we are mistaken if we end there. These things are not the whole of worship. They are not the end, they are only the beginning. If we see no further than the beginning, we may even fail to begin.

We must learn to participate in a free, open, joyous communion of love and praise. Whatever helps this sense of freedom, of openness, I would even say, of *unconstraint,* is going to help the liturgical renewal. Whatever continues to foster rigidity, suspiciousness, timidity, coldness and resentment is going to threaten the liturgical reform with sterility. The great enemy is *constraint,* which brings all these other devils with it.

Let us go back to the *Acts of the Apostles.* The first Christians were people who abounded in irrepressible joy and trust because they realized they were now free and *no longer had to worship under constraint.* Whatever may have been the real qualities of Jewish spirituality at the time, the Christians believed that the Torah required a rigid servitude to forms that had now become empty. The martyrs laid down their lives rather than suffer constraint and obey the official and juridical command to sacrifice to the Roman Emperor. Christian worship in its beginnings is marked by a general, explicit, uncompromising refusal of constraint.

Both progressives and conservatives seem to place their trust in legislation to attain their ends. But liturgical renewal will not be made by laws, and it cannot be prevented by laws. There is danger in the widespread identification of *constraint* with *order*. Obviously, it will do no good simply to constrain progressives to be content with old forms that seem to them lifeless. Just as obviously, those who do not feel or understand the need for renewal cannot be brought into open and living participation merely by constraint.

The progressives do not rely on the force of law in the same way as the conservatives. But even on the progressive side one sometimes feels there is a tendency to exert psychological pressure. The attempt is humanly understandable and I for one do not resent it. But it is a possible source of constraint, and I think this needs to be noted, for it will work against renewal in the long run.

For instance, some rather forceful statements, no doubt substantially correct, have been made insinuating that conservative fears of change might well have a psychoneurotic foundation. Well and good. The fear, the hesitation, the bashfulness-to-the-point-of-panic that characterize some neurotics, and make all forms of communal and interpersonal relationships potentially agonizing to them, obviously do not dispose them to welcome new and strange situations in which they foresee that they will feel threatened. It is quite true that the risks of reform and change will be disturbing to the insecure. But let us remember that too great an eagerness to play on this insecurity and to "punish" the prospective non-participant in advance is not necessarily a sign of perfect psychic balance. There are all kinds of neurotics, and those who project their insecurity on others instead of feeling it themselves are not the ones who are in the best shape.

It is obvious that a situation like this which brings into play the forces of insecurity, of authority, of risk, of change, of law and so on, will naturally create all kinds of inner conflicts, some of which will be felt, others of which will be "acted out" perhaps in a very aggressive and authoritarian fashion by the very ones who are setting themselves up as champions of liberty and of renewal. The insecure will naturally tend to prefer a status quo guaranteed by law and familiar practice, because they depend on knowing what to expect. To point this out to them is no way of winning them over, and let us admit that if the aims of liturgical renewal are to be achieved, such people must be won over reasonably and gently, not bullied into complying.

On the contrary, when a person suffering from anxiety, insecurity and feelings of inferiority concludes that the liturgical movement regards him with suspicion and hostility because he is ill at ease with other people and would rather die than do something new and strange, he feels menaced. He is the object of a great, vague, nameless, limitless, unidentifiable threat. He does not know precisely how he is threatened. He does not know the reason for it. He does not know for sure just what will punish him and for what sin, still less what he can do to appease the hostile forces. All he knows is that because he is what he is (shy, scared, insecure) there are certain people (liturgists) who disapprove of him. They intend to show him up, and liturgy will be their occasion for doing it. He has protected himself and his shyness in worship by approaching God under a comforting anonymity, hitherto guaranteed by inviolable law. Now this trusted protection is going to be brutally and mercilessly removed. He is going to be left defenceless, without any means of understanding his plight or of handling it: and if he cannot handle it he will feel himself for all intents and purposes, excommunicated.

At the same time the aggressive type will be going through a different syndrome. He too is insecure, but he must at all costs prevent himself from seeing and feeling it. He is the one who is never at a loss, always in the forefront, always a leader. Even if he does not really know what he is leading and where he is going, he has to be out in front. Just to make quite sure that no feeling of dissent become conscious, he overplays his role. And so, in the congregation of twelve at a dialogue Mass, he is the one who bellows out the responses, reducing everyone else to a state of tongue-tied embarrassment and spiritual paralysis. This of course comes to his attention. What does he do about it? He falls back on the absolute imperative: he has been asked to participate and he will participate even if it means the end of all spontaneous participation by anybody else and also by himself. He is an absolutist who acts under such constraint that he constrains everyone that comes near him.

Of these two, one might be labeled conservative, the other progressive, but in actual fact there is not too much difference between them in so far as they are both operating under constraint. Now it would be disastrous if the liturgical renewal were to rely on the replacement of one kind of constraint by the other. Renewal means, on the contrary, the replacement of constraint by the openness of simple and joyous participation. Those who have emotional conflicts—and after all, who doesn't?—will do best if they can realize that this openness is practically the only thing that can ease their anxieties in this particular sphere. It will help them, by humility, grace, self-forgetfulness and trust to approach the Lord who will heal them in the relaxed and expanded atmosphere of love which is ideally that of Liturgical Worship.

I say "ideally" because the great problem we face in liturgy today is the temptation to discouragement and resentment which arises when the ideal is not only not promptly realized but not even approximated.

Those whom we may call progressives, whether in liturgy or in the whole field of Catholic renewal, may find themselves pushing forward blindly and recklessly, defying what seems to them an unfair spirit of resistance and inertia on the part of others. The "conservatives" meanwhile—and one regrets to say this—have at times been childishly rebellious to all change and have obstructed even the simplest and most obviously desirable adjustments. (Probably every town has an example of passive resistance and overt recrimination on the part of some Catholic prophet of doom who is now convinced that the Church has become "Protestant" because people pray in English!)

Let us frankly realize that our task is precisely this: to demonstrate our elementary charity and unselfishness—indeed our Christian maturity—by setting aside our own preferences (whether progressive or conservative) in order to arrive at some working formula by which we can all continue to worship as one in Christ. Let us also frankly admit that the tantrums of extremists on both sides are, in most cases, simply childish.

Even well-balanced, sincere and naturally open people may find that the adaptation will not be entirely without struggle. In all social living there has to be a painful dialectic between programs and achievements, ideals and realities, intention and execution. We may start out with a generous response to the program and its demands. We may really open up in all innocence and trust, forgetting that to be open is to be vulnerable. There is no choice, we cannot get into the real inner meaning of participation unless we let our guard down. But if we do, we may find ourselves face to face with someone who has only seemed to let his guard down, and who is still looking for a chance to reinforce his own self-esteem by cutting other people down to size.

In monasteries there is the perennial problem of the novice who comes to choir ready to give his all in the glorious praise of God, and who is quickly and repeatedly made to realize that his contribution is not appreciated. He is caught and ground between the upper millstone of liturgical exhortations from the cantors and the nether millstone of his own energetic incapacity. With his heart wide open, he plunges into cataclysm. After six months, he is reduced to frustrated silence, or sings in a miserable, self-pitying falsetto for the rest of his life, lost to renewal, to progress, to liturgy and to anything else but the well-tried spirituality of cloistered victimhood.

What is to be done about such problems? There is no magic answer. But one thing is certain. If all our ardor and attention are concentrated on a liturgical *ideal*, then we will inevitably end by hurting, punishing and unnecessarily constraining the poor well-meaning flesh and blood individual who takes our exhortation seriously, and generously tries to give us what we seem to be asking. Let us think of ideals, but also, above all, of people—not people in the abstract but the ones with whom we worship.

If we are going to ask limited human beings to participate in the liturgy, then we must be content for a while with the imperfect participation we are going to get. It is not always going to be wonderful. It is probably going to be in some ways much less tranquil and edifying than the comparative order and serenity of the "old mass." The new liturgy may be in many ways a relief—but it is not necessarily going to attain at once to perfect harmony, order and beauty. Let us not make things worse by insisting that everything we attempt is at once "perfect"!

One thing that will inevitably aggravate the sense of constraint is the fact that the liturgy continues to be our official public prayer, authoritative and precisely regulated. It makes severe demands, not only on the feelings, the imagination and the understanding of the participant, not only on his heart and will, but even on his conscience. One of the agonizing things about the liturgy, for certain priests, is the exaggerated fear of making mistakes and therefore of being guilty. This "rubrical paralysis" is what accounts for the ugliness and impropriety of so many Masses. Do not blame the poor priest!

God alone understands the depth of his unspoken tribula-
tion. The fault lies probably with the seminaries. The mere
changing of Laws does nothing to remedy this situation. On
the contrary, it creates new problems: one finds himself trying to fulfil new obligations which he does not yet properly
understand . . .

By now, however, all of us have probably made enough
mistakes in the "new Mass" to realize first of all that it is not
just a matter of being rubrically correct. And also all of us have
had to make special adjustments to meet a special situation so
that, without being "innovators" exactly, we have at least had
to interpret the new rubrics in a reasonable and constructive
personal way. Hence the complaints of parishioners who de-
plore the fact that "every pastor has a different way of doing
things" are not really to be taken seriously. If these people had
lived in the Middle Ages, to which they perhaps think they
look back with nostalgia, they would have found far more re-
gional differences and apparent inconsistencies than they will
ever see in twentieth century Catholicism. In fact one might
say that medieval Catholicism, as it *really* was, manifested in
some areas a spirit of freedom that we would do well to recap-
ture if we could. (I hasten to add that not *all* the clerical freedom of the Middle Ages was worthy of imitation.)

The liturgical renewal is going to demand a great deal of
experimentation. But how can we experiment under juridical
constraint? It would seem that much of the renewal will have
to be carried on in a spirit of informality and freedom, to some
extent outside the framework of formal liturgical worship.
The dry mass, for instance, and the informal prayer vigil offer
many possibilities of free experiment, one would almost say of
improvisation, which would be out of the question in formal liturgical service or in the administration of the Sacraments.

One last thought: the open approach in liturgy is perhaps
forever beyond the capacity of those of us who have grown old
in "closed" and rigid forms. But there are children. They will
be in any case the ones to benefit from the liturgical reform.

Why not let them, in the simplicity and inspired spontaneity which are their special gift, and guided by sensitive and alert adults, begin to sketch out the creative and original forms of the future liturgy for which we are all waiting?

I make this suggestion seriously, and without a trace of sentiment. Naturally I have no clear idea how it might be done. But childhood *is* the age of openness, simplicity, spontaneity, and honesty. Of course, today's child has been influenced by TV, and his openness has been tampered with in many other subtle ways.

There is much hope for liturgical renewal if it can somehow be carried out in a spirit of *play*. Play is not flippant or inconsequential. It is a very serious and very necessary activity. It is in play that the human heart is at once open, engaged, joyous, serious and self-forgetful. The open, thoughtless, hieratic self-forgetfulness of play is more likely than anything else to provide a substitute for the self-concerned engrossment of subjective concentration that has so far provided the worshipper with his chief ground for seriousness in worship.

If our own children cannot help us discover a new liturgy, perhaps the new nations, the more primitive societies which are the children in the family of nations, will be the ones to lead us into the world of renewal. The African monasteries of Cistercians and Benedictines have already petitioned the Holy See for permission to use native instruments (especially drums) in their worship.

One thing that is certain to come out of Africa is the revival of the ancient liturgical art of *the dance,* traditionally a problem to western Christianity. This of course opens up tempting avenues of speculation. But it must be said that the world today needs forms of worship that are dynamic, colorful, rhythmic and full of disciplined and expressive movement. Whatever may be the outcome, it is in that direction that the success of full liturgical participation really lies.

[1964]

NOTES

Time and the Liturgy

1. Gunther Anders has coined this striking expression to describe the change of perspective that followed the dropping of the first Atomic Bomb on Hiroshima. We are now living in an age in which we *know* that the world can at any moment be rendered practically uninhabitable, and mankind obliterated. Yet in a very real sense this consciousness was already that of the first Christians. One is tempted to speculate on the profound effect the Christian eschatological concept of time has had on all subsequent developments in thought and science.

The Sacrament of Advent in the Spirituality of St. Bernard

1. Serm. iv, Adv. n.i.
2. Peritura sectantes amittunt solida quibus apprehensis emergere et salvare possent animas suas. Serm. i, Adv. n.i.
3. Neque enim tam devote Ecclesia universa praesentem celebraret Adventum, nisi lateret in eo ALIQUOD MAGNUM SACRAMENTUM. Serm. i, Adv. n.i.

4. Eph. 1:9–10.
5. Col. 1:12.
6. Cf. John 17:23. I in them and Thou in me that they may be made perfect in one and that the world may know that Thou hast sent me and hast loved them as Thou hast also loved me.
7. Serm. vii, n.ii.
8. Serm. vii, n.i.
9. Rom. 8:31.
10. Ad hoc ipsum venit in mundum, ut habitans in hominibus, cum hominibus, pro hominibus, et tenebras nostras illuminaret, et labores levaret, et peric ulapropulsaret. Serm. vii, n.ii.
11. Cf. Col. 1:18–23, 2:12–15, 3:1–5. But especially Eph. 1:18, 2:8.
12. Christus enim qui descendit ipse est qui ascendit ut adimpleret omnia. Serm. i, n.vi.
13. Eph. 2:5–6, Col. 2:12.
14. Rom. 6:4.
15. Serm. iv, Adv., n.i.
16. Spiritual Canticle B, xxvii, n.i.
17. Col. 3:1.
18. Serm. i, Adv., n.vi.
19. E. Gilson, *Mystical Theology of St. Bernard.*
20. Serm. i, Adv., n.viii.
21. Rom. 10:6–8.
22. Rom. 10:10.
23. Eph. 3:17.
24. Eph. 3:19.
25. Eph. 3:16, Rom. 5:5.
26. Gal. 4:6.
27. Gal. 4:9, cf. II Cor. 1:22.
28. II Cor. 4:17.
29. Gal. 4:9.
30. Gal. 6:2.
31. Serm. i, Adv. n.x; cf. Serm. vi, Adv., n.ii.

32. Serm. ii, Adv., n.iii.
33. Serm. iv in Vig. Nat., n.ii.
34. Serm. iv in Vig. Nat., n.i.
35. *Ibid.* n.iv.
36. Serm. iii, Adv., n.i.
37. John 3:16–19.
38. John 3:19, 12:46, 8:12.
39. John 4:42.
40. Serm. iv, Adv. n.iii.
41. Serm. ii, Adv. n.i.
42. Job 5:13.
43. Rom. 10:6–8.
44. Serm. ii, Adv. n.i.
45. Serm. ii, Adv. n.i.
46. Molestus est ergo non solum hominibus sed etiam Deo quisquis nec majestatem cogitat in timore nec charitatem cum amore meditatur. Serm. ii, Adv. n.i.
47. Serm. iv, Adv. n.i.
48. Canticle 2:6.
49. Phil. 3:21.
50. Serm. iv, Adv. nn.iv–vii.
51. Cf. Serm. vi, Adv. n.i.
52. Felix conscientia in qua luctamen hujusmodi indesipenter conficitur, donec quod mortale est absorbeatur a vita, donec evacuetur timor quod ex parte est et succedat laetitia quod perfectum est. Serm. iii, Vig. Nat. n.v.
53. Serm. v, Adv. n.i.
54. Per virtutem enim pervenitur ad gloriam quia Dominus virtutum ipse est rex gloriae. Serm. v, Adv. n.i.
55. Serm. iv, Adv. n.iii.
56. Serm. iii, Adv. n.iv.
57. Serm. iii, Adv. nn.iv–vii.
58. Tantum dicamus iniquitates nostras et justificabit nos gratis, ut gratia commendetur. Serm. iii, Adv. n.vii.
59. Delectabiliter dormiunt (in medio Adventu) qui eum norunt. Serm. v, Adv. n.i.

60. Gal. 5:6.
61. Rom. 10:16.
62. Serm. v, Adv. n.ii.
63. Psalm 118:11.
64. I Cor. 8:1.
65. Serm. v, Adv. n.ii.
66. Serm. v, Adv. n.iii.
67. Serm. iii, Adv. n.ii.
68. Serm. iii, Adv. n.ii.
69. Hom. i, Sup. Missus Est, n.i.
70. Hom. i, Sup. Missus Est, n.i.
71. Hom. iv, Sup. Missus Est, n.viii.
72. Serm. ii, Adv. n.v.
73. Serm. ii, Adv. n.v.
74. Hom. ii, Sup. Missus Est, n.xvii.
75. Cf. Serm. xiv de Diversis and the final Sermons in Cantica.
76. De Gradibus Humilitatis et Superbiae, n.x. ff.
77. Hom. ii, Sup. Missus Est, n.iii.
78. Hom. iii, Sup. Missus Est, n.vi.
79. Serm. xl in Cantica, n.iv.
80. Hom. ii, Sup. Missus Est, n.vii.
81. Ibid.
82. Hom. ii, Sup. Missus Est, nn.iv–vii.
83. Hom. ii, Sup. Missus Est, n.xi.
84. Hom. iii, Sup. Missus Est, n.iv.
85. Hom. iii, Sup. Missus Est, n.iv.

The Name of the Lord

1. C. Von Rad. *Old Testament Theology*, New York, 1962, Vol. 1, p. 183.
2. Ibid., p. 186.
3. Ibid., p. 183.
4. See the article of G. Lambert, S.J., "Que Signifie le Nom Divin YHWH," *Nouvelle Revue Theologique*, 1952, No. 9, p. 897 ff.

5. Th. C. Vriezen, *An Outline of Old Testament Theology,* Oxford, 1960, p. 195.

Thomas Merton (1915–1968) is widely acclaimed as one of the most influential spiritual masters of the twentieth century. A monk, poet, spiritual writer, and social activist, he is perhaps best known for his spiritual autobiography, *The Seven Storey Mountain.*

Ave Maria Press, a ministry of the Congregation of Holy Cross,
is a Catholic publishing company that serves the spiritual and formative
needs of the Church and its schools, institutions, and ministers; Christian
individuals and families; and others seeking spiritual nourishment.

For a complete listing of titles, visit www.avemariapress.com

 ave maria press

The original imprint for books on
Catholic prayer and spirituality.

 SORIN BOOKS

Launched in 1999, the Sorin Books
imprint publishes books on personal
growth, relationships, and family life for
the general spiritual seeker.

 Forest of Peace

Acquired in 2003, this imprint showcases
the innovative spiritual vision of Edward
Hays, popular author of *Prayers for a
Planetary Pilgrim* and *Prayers for the
Domestic Church*.

 Christian Classics

This esteemed imprint, founded forty
years ago and acquired in 2003, publishes
classic works of the Christian heritage.

Ave Maria Press
and its imprints
publish many titles in
the following areas:

Prayer

Spirituality

Pastoral Ministry

Theology

Religious Education

ave maria press
Notre Dame, IN 46556
Ph: 800.282.1865
www.avemariapress.com
A Ministry of the Indiana Province of Holy Cross

PROMO CODE: FH8Ø6Ø917A8